# DESIDERIUS ERASMUS

# SPIRITUAL LEADERS AND THINKERS

JOHN CALVIN

DALAI LAMA (TENZIN GYATSO)

MARY BAKER EDDY

JONATHAN EDWARDS

DESIDERIUS ERASMUS

MOHANDAS GANDHI

AYATOLLAH RUHOLLAH KHOMEINI

MARTIN LUTHER

AIMEE SEMPLE McPHERSON

THOMAS MERTON

SRI SATYA SAI BABA

ELISABETH SCHÜSSLER FIORENZA

EMANUEL SWEDENBORG

SPIRITUAL
LEADERS AND
THINKERS

# DESIDERIUS ERASMUS

Samuel Willard Crompton

Introductory Essay by
**Martin E. Marty, Professor Emeritus**
University of Chicago Divinity School

CHELSEA HOUSE
PUBLISHERS
A Haights Cross Communications Company

Philadelphia

COVER: Portrait of Desiderius Erasmus by Hans Holbein the younger (1497–1543).


CHELSEA HOUSE PUBLISHERS

VP, NEW PRODUCT DEVELOPMENT  Sally Cheney
DIRECTOR OF PRODUCTION  Kim Shinners
CREATIVE MANAGER  Takeshi Takahashi
MANUFACTURING MANAGER  Diann Grasse

**Staff for DESIDERIUS ERASMUS**

EXECUTIVE EDITOR  Lee Marcott
EDITOR  Kate Sullivan
PRODUCTION EDITOR  Noelle Nardone
PHOTO EDITOR  Sarah Bloom
SERIES AND COVER DESIGNER  Keith Trego
LAYOUT  21st Century Publishing and Communications, Inc.

A Haights Cross Communications ◤ Company

www.chelseahouse.com

First Printing

9 8 7 6 5 4 3 2 1

Library of Congress Cataloging-in-Publication Data

Crompton, Samuel Willard.
    Desiderius Erasmus / Samuel Willard Crompton.
      p. cm.—(Spiritual leaders and thinkers)
Includes bibliographical references and index.
    ISBN 0-7910-8101-X
    1. Erasmus, Desiderius, d. 1536. 2. Reformation—Biography. I. Title. II. Series.
BR350.E7C75 2004
282'.092—dc22

                                            2004011113

All links and web addresses were checked and verified at the time of publication. Due to the dynamic nature of the web, some addresses and links may have changed since publication and may no longer be valid.

# CONTENTS

# Foreword

Why become acquainted with notable people when making efforts to understand the religions of the world?

Most of the faith communities number hundreds of millions of people. What can attention paid to one tell about more, if not most, to say nothing of *all*, their adherents? Here is why:

The people in this series are exemplars. If you permit me to take a little detour through medieval dictionaries, their role will become clear.

In medieval lexicons, the word *exemplum* regularly showed up with a peculiar definition. No one needs to know Latin to see that it relates to "example" and "exemplary." But back then, *exemplum* could mean something very special.

That "ex-" at the beginning of such words signals "taking out" or "cutting out" something or other. Think of to "excise" something, which is to snip it out. So, in the more interesting dictionaries, an *exemplum* was referred to as "a clearing in the woods," something cut out of the forests.

These religious figures are *exempla*, figurative clearings in the woods of life. These clearings and these people perform three functions:

First, they define. You can be lost in the darkness, walking under the leafy canopy, above the undergrowth, plotless in the pathless forest. Then you come to a clearing. It defines with a sharp line: there, the woods end; here, the open space begins.

Great religious figures are often stumblers in the dark woods.

We see them emerging in the bright light of the clearing, blinking, admitting that they had often been lost in the mysteries of existence, tangled up with the questions that plague us all, wandering without definition. Then they discover the clearing, and, having done so, they point our way to it. We then learn more of who we are and where we are. Then we can set our own direction.

Second, the *exemplum*, the clearing in the woods of life, makes possible a brighter vision. Great religious pioneers in every case experience illumination and then they reflect their light into the hearts and minds of others. In Buddhism, a key word is *enlightenment*. In the Bible, "the people who walked in darkness have seen a great light." They see it because their prophets or savior brought them to the sun in the clearing.

Finally, when you picture a clearing in the woods, an *exemplum*, you are likely to see it as a place of cultivation. Whether in the Black Forest of Germany, on the American frontier, or in the rain forests of Brazil, the clearing is the place where, with light and civilization, residents can cultivate, can produce culture. As an American moviegoer, my mind's eye remembers cinematic scenes of frontier days and places that pioneers hacked out of the woods. There, they removed stones, planted, built a cabin, made love and produced families, smoked their meat, hung out laundered clothes, and read books. All that can happen in clearings.

In the case of these religious figures, planting and cultivating and harvesting are tasks in which they set an example and then inspire or ask us to follow. Most of us would not have the faintest idea how to find or be found by God, to nurture the Holy Spirit, to create a philosophy of life without guidance. It is not likely that most of us would be satisfied with our search if we only consulted books of dogma or philosophy, though such may come to have their place in the clearing.

Philosopher Søren Kierkegaard properly pointed out that you cannot learn to swim by being suspended from the ceiling on a belt and reading a "How To" book on swimming. You learn because a parent or an instructor plunges you into water, supports you when necessary, teaches you breathing and motion, and then releases you to swim on your own.

Kierkegaard was not criticizing the use of books. I certainly have nothing against books. If I did, I would not be commending this series to you, as I am doing here. For guidance and courage in the spiritual quest, or—and this is by no means unimportant!—in intellectual pursuits, involving efforts to understand the paths others have taken, there seems to be no better way than to follow a fellow mortal, but a man or woman of genius, depth, and daring. We "see" them through books like these.

Exemplars come in very different styles and forms. They bring differing kinds of illumination, and then suggest or describe diverse patterns of action to those who join them. In the case of the present series, it is possible for someone to repudiate or disagree with *all* the religious leaders in this series. It is possible also to be nonreligious and antireligious and therefore to disregard the truth claims of all of them. It is more difficult, however, to ignore them. Atheists, agnostics, adherents, believers, and fanatics alike live in cultures that are different for the presence of these people. "Leaders and thinkers" they may be, but most of us do best to appraise their thought in the context of the lives they lead or have led.

If it is possible to reject them all, it is impossible to affirm everything that all of them were about. They disagree with each other, often in basic ways. Sometimes they develop their positions and ways of thinking by separating themselves from all the others. If they met each other, they would likely judge each other cruelly. Yet the lives of each and all of them make a contribution to the intellectual and spiritual quests of those who go in ways other than theirs. There are tens of thousands of religions in the world, and millions of faith communities. Every one of them has been shaped by founders and interpreters, agents of change and prophets of doom or promise. It may seem arbitrary to walk down a bookshelf and let a finger fall on one or another, almost accidentally. This series may certainly look arbitrary in this way. Why precisely the choice of these exemplars?

In some cases, it is clear that the publishers have chosen someone who has a constituency. Many of the world's 54 million Lutherans may be curious about where they got their name, who the man Martin Luther was. Others are members of a community but choose isolation: The hermit monk Thomas Merton is typical. Still others are exiled and achieve their work far from the clearing in which they grew up; here the Dalai Lama is representative. Quite a number of the selected leaders had been made unwelcome, or felt unwelcome in the clearings, in their own childhoods and youth. This reality has almost always been the case with women like Mary Baker Eddy or Aimee Semple McPherson. Some are extremely controversial: Ayatollah Ruhollah Khomeini stands out. Yet to read of this life and thought as one can in this series will be illuminating in much of the world of conflict today.

Reading of religious leaders can be a defensive act: Study the lives of certain ones among them and you can ward off spiritual—and sometimes even militant—assaults by people who follow them. Reading and learning can be a personally positive act: Most of these figures led lives that we can indeed call exemplary. Such lives can throw light on communities of people who are in no way tempted to follow them. I am not likely to be drawn to the hermit life, will not give up my allegiance to medical doctors, or be successfully nonviolent. Yet Thomas Merton reaches me and many non-Catholics in our communities; Mary Baker Eddy reminds others that there are more ways than one to approach healing; Mohandas Gandhi stings the conscience of people in cultures like ours where resorting to violence is too frequent, too easy.

Finally, reading these lives tells something about how history is made by imperfect beings. None of these subjects is a god, though some of them claimed that they had special access to the divine, or that they were like windows that provided for illumination to that which is eternal. Most of their stories began with inauspicious childhoods. Sometimes they were victimized, by parents or by leaders of religions from which they later broke.

Some of them were unpleasant and abrasive. They could be ungracious toward those who were near them and impatient with laggards. If their lives were symbolic clearings, places for light, many of them also knew clouds and shadows and the fall of night. How they met the challenges of life and led others to face them is central to the plot of all of them.

I have often used a rather unexciting concept to describe what I look for in books: *interestingness*. The authors of these books, one might say, had it easy, because the characters they treat are themselves so interesting. But the authors also had to be interesting and responsible. If, as they wrote, they would have dulled the personalities of their bright characters, that would have been a flaw as marring as if they had treated their subjects without combining fairness and criticism, affection and distance. To my eye, and I hope in yours, they take us to spiritual and intellectual clearings that are so needed in our dark times.

Martin E. Marty
The University of Chicago

# 1

# Summons
# from England

esiderius Erasmus was in Rome in the spring of 1509. The consummate scholar and man of letters had been in Italy for the last three years, translating, editing, and spending time in Venice with his printer, the esteemed Aldus Manutius. Sometime in the summer of 1509, Erasmus received a letter from William Blount, Lord Mountjoy of England. Blount, who had been a friend and patron to Erasmus in the past, gave Erasmus the exciting news that King Henry VII had passed away and had been succeeded by his son, 18-year-old King Henry VIII. Blount was enthusiastic:

> I am quite sure, my dear Erasmus, that, the moment you heard
> that our sovereign lord, Henry the Eighth, had succeeded to
> the throne on his father's death, every particle of gloom
> left your heart. For you are bound to repose the highest of
> hopes in a prince whose exceptional and almost more than
> human talents you know so well, particularly since you are not
> merely his acquaintance but his friend.[1]

Erasmus, who was Dutch by birth, had stayed in England between 1499 and 1500. During that time, he had made the acquaintance of Henry VIII, then Prince Henry, and the two had developed a long-distance friendship based on their mutual love of Latin scholarship. The young Henry was a far cry from the bloated tyrant he later became as king. In his youth, Henry Tudor was handsome, scholarly, and well liked. William Blount went on to describe how the old king's death and the new king's accession had brought joy to England:

> Oh, Erasmus, if you could only see how happily excited every-
> one is here, and how all are congratulating themselves on their
> prince's greatness, and how they pray above all for his long life,
> you would be bound to weep for joy! Heaven smiles, earth
> rejoices; all is milk and honey and nectar. Tight-fistedness is
> well and truly banished. Generosity scatters wealth with
> unstinting hand.[2]

The expression "tight-fistedness" was a glancing reference to the deceased King Henry VII. He had been known for unremitting thriftiness, to the point of being a miser. Now, his son appeared ready to open the coffers to men of merit, like Erasmus:

> Our King's heart is set not upon gold or jewels or mines of ore, but upon virtue, reputation, and eternal renown. Here is a mere sample: a few days ago, when he said that he longed to be a more accomplished scholar, I remarked, "We do not expect this of you; what we do expect is that you should foster and encourage those who are scholars." "Of course," he replied, "for without them we could scarcely exist." What better remark could be made by any king?[3]

Blount's letter set Erasmus thinking. He had been in Italy for three years, and he had accomplished much good work. He had published a new version of his famous *Adages* and was well along in his study of Greek. Unfortunately, he had failed to find a good and lasting patron, someone who could remove from him the burden of earning his daily bread. Lack of money had been a constant theme in Erasmus's life up to this point. Perhaps William Blount was suggesting that King Henry VIII would now become the long-sought-after patron. Indeed, William Blount closed his letter with an earnest request for Erasmus to come to England:

> I am distressed to hear that you have fallen sick in Italy. You know that I never pressed you to go to Italy, but now that I observe the literary experience and personal reputation you have acquired there I am very sorry not to have accompanied you; for my belief is that such a high degree of scholarship is worth the price of hunger, poverty, and illness, even death itself. Enclosed with this letter you will find a bill of exchange for the money. So look after your health and come back to us as soon as you can. Yours with all his being, William Mountjoy.[4]

Erasmus may well have grimaced as he read these words. What did Lord Mountjoy or any other English lord know about hunger or poverty? They had never been forced to beg for their pay as Erasmus had. The more he thought about it, the more Erasmus was convinced that it was time to leave Italy. He had gone there seeking the humanistic scholarship of the day and the manuscripts that provided access to the great learning of early Christian times. He had found both and had done his best to profit from them. Now it was time to return to northern Europe.

Erasmus, however, had a bitter memory of England. During his year in the island kingdom, Erasmus had earned what came to about 20 pounds sterling, a large amount for such an impoverished scholar and a sum he planned to take with him to Paris. Neither William Blount nor anyone else had warned Erasmus that the miserly King Henry VII had created a new law, one that forbade the departure of currency from England. The customs inspectors at Dover had taken away about 18 of Erasmus's 20 pounds, and the bitterness from this loss still lingered. Perhaps this was why William Blount had so fervently described the new king as a man with open pockets (to learn more about this monarch, enter the keywords "King Henry VII England" into any Internet search engine and browse the listed sites).

Now, a year later, Erasmus made his way north across the Italian Alps. He rode on horseback with two or three companions. As he left Italy, Erasmus began to write, on horseback, the first words of what would become his most famous book, *The Praise of Folly*. Perhaps he knew that his decision to leave Italy and go to England was folly. Or perhaps he knew that the best efforts of human beings often go astray. In any case, he penned the opening words to what became one of the first best-selling books of modern times (it remains in print to this very day):

> At what rate so ever the world talks of me (for I am not ignorant what an ill report Folly has got, even among the most foolish), yet that I am that she, that only she, whose deity recreates both gods and men, even this is a sufficient argument, that I no sooner stepped up to speak to this full assembly than all your faces put on a kind of new and unwonted pleasantness.[5]

Erasmus had launched upon the greatest literary venture of his career. His name would remain permanently entwined with the Goddess of Folly.

# 2

# Erasmus, His Brother, and the Brethren

*" . . . there is nothing on earth more pleasant or sweeter than loving and being loved, so there is, in my opinion, nothing more distressing or miserable than living without being loved in return . . . "*

—Erasmus, in a letter to his friend Servatius

M uch controversy surrounds the early years of Desiderius Erasmus. The controversy exists because Erasmus spent much of his adult life trying to escape from his humble and painful origins. He never wanted to be reminded that he, the son of a priest, was born out of wedlock.

The facts of Erasmus's early years are hazy at best. Erasmus often cited the year 1466 when asked about the year of his birth, but some evidence points instead to the year 1469. The place of his birth is also a matter of dispute. Erasmus later called himself "Erasmus of Rotterdam," but evidence suggests that he was actually born in nearby Gouda. In either case, we can safely assume that Erasmus was born in the late 1460s, somewhere near the heart of old Holland.

Today, we often use the word "Holland" to describe what is properly titled the Kingdom of the Netherlands. This is because many people are familiar with Holland as a place of wooden shoes, comfortable and snug houses, and dykes and dams used to hold back the sea. All these stereotypes have some basis in fact, and Holland has provided much of the character that later became the center of Dutch, or Netherlandish, culture.

One stereotype that has come down to us is of the Dutch being sturdy, self-reliant people. They bravely reclaimed their land from the sea, and they built dykes and dams that became the wonder of the engineering world. It would be pleasant to think that Erasmus venerated his Dutch upbringing, but he did not. Later in life, he poured scorn on the country of his youth, describing its people as boorish and lacking in literary culture. If this seems like serious ingratitude, one has to remember that Erasmus spent the most lonely and poverty-stricken years of his life in Holland.

**FAMILY HISTORY**

His father was a priest named Gerhard (his surname is not known). Almost nothing is known about him except that he was man of some learning who treasured his Latin books above all else. The priest must have passed this trait on to his son, for Erasmus always cherished books above all his other possessions.

Erasmus's mother was named Margaret (again, there is no surname recorded). She took care of Erasmus and his older brother, Peter, until Erasmus was about 13. Then she died of the plague, leaving the two boys to their own fate. Their father had apparently disappeared. Erasmus almost never mentioned his mother, either in his letters or otherwise. Perhaps the memory was too painful for him to summon up; perhaps he felt she had been a disappointment as a mother. Whatever the story, we know even less about Margaret than we do about Gerhard. The question that has sparked more interest is how a Roman Catholic priest could have fathered a child.

The situation was more common than people in the modern world might think. By about 1450, Europe had become more secular and less religious than it had been 100 years earlier. Many people expressed dissatisfaction with the Roman Catholic Church, which had been rocked by scandals surrounding worldly popes and councils. More than a few churchmen, even pious ones, took concubines or wives.

Whether he was born in 1466 or 1469, Erasmus entered the world in one of the less prestigious regions of Europe. Holland had been governed by its counts for generations, but the counts owed allegiance either to France or to the Holy Roman Empire, which corresponded roughly to modern Germany. Holland was therefore a province, and it sometimes changed hands when different dynasties intermarried. The Dutch were an independent people in spirit, but in practical fact, they were subjects of the count who was, in turn, a subject of the king or emperor.

## THE BRETHREN OF THE COMMON LIFE

Erasmus and his brother Peter became public wards after their mother's death. The two were given into the care of a religious group called the Brethren of the Common Life. Founded in Holland about 100 years earlier, the Brethren differed from other monastic orders in that its members did not take solemn vows— they could always choose to leave the Brethren. In other ways, however, the Brethren followed the same strict code that most monastic orders observed. Members swore to chastity, poverty, and obedience. Neither Erasmus nor his brother was pleased to be part of this ascetic brotherhood that chose to deny the world.

One of the earliest of Erasmus's letters that has been preserved was sent to his older brother. Even though they lived close to each other, the brothers wrote far more often than people do today; this was their primary method of communication. In the letter, Erasmus accused his brother of neglecting him:

> Have you so completely rid yourself of all brotherly feeling, or has all thought of your Erasmus wholly fled your heart? I write letters and send them repeatedly, I demand news again and again. I keep asking your friends when they come from your direction, but they never have a hint of a letter or any message; they merely say that you are well. Of course this is the most welcome news I could hear but you are now more dutiful thereby. As I perceive how obstinate you are, I believe it would be easier to get blood from a stone than coax a letter out of you.[6]

While he implored his brother to communicate more frequently and more fully, he also emphasized how much his brother meant to him:

> If you desire to know what I am about, I love you intensely, as you deserve; your name is on my lips and in my heart; I think of you and speak of you often with my friends, but none more often more intimately, or pleasantly than with Servatius, our fellow-countryman.[7]

There is no record of an answer. We hear almost nothing of Erasmus's brother after this, and can only wonder whether there was some reason for their separation. Was there some great wound or hardness between them? Historians do not know.

By 1487, when Erasmus wrote this letter, his familial relations had all but disappeared. His mother was dead, his father's fate was unknown, and his brother had turned away from him. When later in life Erasmus seemed suspicious of human nature or mistrustful of friends, one must remember that his youth was filled with the pain of separation.

It was in the care of the Brethren of the Common Life that Erasmus and his brother received their earliest education, but Erasmus remained a skeptic concerning the Brethren throughout his life. Although it is possible that the Brethren's type of voluntary monasticism might have appealed to him, he was much disappointed by the type of Latin he learned at the monastery and despaired of the methods of instruction. It is also likely that he received his share of beatings at the monastery during his youth. Later in his life, Erasmus would be among the first in Christian Europe to call for more humane and intelligent methods of education.

Erasmus also suffered disappointment with his guardians. His father, Gerhard, had left behind a library of books written in Latin that were worth a handy sum of money. The books were probably loose folio pages rather than true bound books, as we know them today. Gerhard left the valuable books in the hands of three guardians. Chief among the three was Peter Winckel, one of Erasmus's schoolmasters. In a letter from Erasmus to Peter Winckel, Erasmus wrote of his concerns over the books and the money they could bring:

> I am very much afraid that the end of this brief period may find our affairs not yet safely taken care of, though they should have been settled long since—belatedly even then. Therefore I think that all ingenuity, care and zeal should be devoted to seeing that our [Erasmus and his brother] interests are not harmed. Perhaps you will say that I am one of the kind who worry in case the sky should fall. This might be true enough if the capital were already there, waiting in our pockets. But your practical good sense will take special care to see that our property is accounted for. The books have still to be offered for sale, still to seek a buyer, still to catch a glimpse of a bidder.[8]

Knowing as we do that Erasmus was to become one of the

greatest letter writers and authors of all time, we might expect that he would have wanted to keep the books rather than sell them. History teaches, however, that Erasmus was always concerned about money.

Erasmus's hopes were dashed once more. Though their father's library was eventually sold, the profits were not sufficient to provide either Erasmus or his brother with a financially independent future. As a result, both brothers entered monasteries: Erasmus at around the age of 18 and his brother at about 21.

Many years later, Erasmus wrote one of his *Colloquies* on the subject of "Rash Vows," the perhaps too-eager decision to enter the monastic life. Partly autobiographical and partly universal in nature, this excerpted conversation illustrates the dilemma experienced by Erasmus and many other young men of his time:

> **Arnoldus:** O! Cornelius, well met heartily, you have been lost this hundred years.
>
> **Cornelius:** What my old companion Arnoldus, the man I longed to see most of any man in the world! God save you.
>
> **Arnoldus:** We all gave thee over for lost. But prithee where hast been rambling all this while?
>
> **Cornelius:** In t'other world.
>
> **Arnoldus:** Why truly a body would think so by thy slovenly dress, lean carcass, and ghastly [physique].
>
> **Cornelius:** Well, but I am just come from Jerusalem, not from the Stygian Shades.
>
> **Arnoldus:** What wind blew thee thither?
>
> **Cornelius:** What wind blows a great many other folks thither?
>
> **Arnoldus:** Why Folly, or else I am mistaken.[9]

The reader learns that Arnoldus had committed a similar error. He has gone on pilgrimage, to Rome and Compostella, and has found nothing but disappointment in the process. When

Cornelius asks what compelled Arnoldus to go on pilgrimage, Arnoldus indicates that alcohol played a role in his decision:

> There was a knot of neighbors of us drinking together, and when the wine began to work in our noodles, one said he had a mind to make a visit to St. James, and another to St. Peter; presently there was one or two that promised to go with them, till at last it was concluded upon to go all together; and I, that I might not seem a disagreeable companion, rather than break good company, promised to go too. The next question was, whether we should go to Rome or Compostella? Upon the debate it was determined that we should all, God willing, set out the next day for both places.[10]

Perhaps Erasmus exaggerated somewhat in telling his story, but we know that medieval Europeans did undertake pilgrimages for a host of different reasons (to learn more about this custom, enter the keywords "medieval pilgrimages" into any Internet search engine and browse the listed sites). Perhaps they entered monasteries for a similar reasons, not all of which were truly appropriate for choosing religious life.

## THE AUGUSTINIAN MONASTERY AT STEYN

Erasmus entered the Augustinian monastery at Steyn, not far from Gouda. There he found a more traditional monastic life than what he had known among the Brethren of the Common Life. Here again, however, Erasmus was disappointed by scholarship limited by inadequate resources. The Augustinians venerated the early Christian authors but generally read rather poor translations of their works. From his early scholastic experiences, Erasmus developed a powerful desire to see the early, original sources for the Christian faith.

While he was with the Augustinians, Erasmus developed powerful friendships. He had been terribly lonely throughout his youth; now he was among other young men who appreciated literature and "high thinking." He exchanged numerous letters with many of his fellow monks, but the one on whom he fastened his affections was Servatius Rogerus. The two young men developed a close friendship, although Erasmus's emotions were too much for Servatius to handle. Before long, Erasmus was writing letters to this effect:

> My dear Servatius, as there is nothing on earth more pleasant or sweeter than loving and being loved, so there is, in my opinion, nothing more distressing or more miserable than living without being loved in return; and likewise, as there is nothing more worthy of humanity than to return the love of him who loves us, so too there is nothing more inhuman, or closer to the state of wild beasts than to shun, not to say dislike, one who loves us.[11]

In this correspondence, we hear the voice of rhetoric. Erasmus had already become a master of the letter, or essay, and these words are more theoretical musings than his intimate thoughts. Erasmus's true, personal desperation emerges just a paragraph later:

> I have left untried no means by which the youthful heart could be affected, but you remain steadfastly of your former mind, harder than adamant. What can I promise myself, unhappy man that I am? What hope remains? Am I, like Sisyphus, once again with useless toil to roll a stone uphill?[12]

Later in the letter, Erasmus resigned himself to fate:

> 'Tis hard, but patience makes to bear/Whatever can not be righted.' And yet, dear Servatius, though you have now forgotten, to put it rather mildly, your friend Erasmus, still he remembers and shall remember his friend Servatius so long as he remembers himself, or the breath shall inhabit his frame.[13]

Servatius kept Erasmus at a distance from this point onward. Erasmus came to realize that the monastery would not provide the home, shelter, and friendship that he had longed for his entire life. The realization made him a different man.

From about 1488 or 1489 onward, the tone of Erasmus's letters changed. He never again pleaded for acceptance in the way he had begged Servatius; a cooler and more neutral tone emerged in his writings. Erasmus's heart was clearly broken, and he would never risk it in the same way again. He did, however, continue to cultivate friendship.

As Erasmus's letters to Servatius tailed off, his letters to another friend, Cornelis Gerard, began to multiply. Erasmus kept a much better distance with Cornelis than he had with Servatius, and the two men exchanged numerous letters flattering one another on their scholastic achievements. Sometime in 1489, Cornelis wrote:

> To the Consummate Scholar, Erasmus,
>
> Your lavish kindness, dear Erasmus, reveals itself on all hands, and it has placed me under strong obligation to you by a service that will not be forgotten. For you have consented to what I long ago requested and shall always continue eagerly to demand—such is your unrivalled good will and innate amiability. You did it of your own free will too, and even more did more than I requested. You say in your letter—and I cannot believe that you wrote without meaning it— that nothing has given you more pleasure than the fact that you and I are joined in our studies and compensate for our separation by frequent correspondence. All this, dear Erasmus, raises my love for you to a high pitch, and I shall converse with you unfailingly and often by means of letters; and rightly too.[14]

Clearly, Erasmus had found a more congenial friend than Servatius. Erasmus's letters, however, while acclaiming his new friend, also complained at length about the form of education and the books available at the monastery. He was mired, he said, "knee deep in the excrement of Scholasticism."

### THE FAILURE OF THE SCHOLASTIC MOVEMENT

Scholasticism, or the Scholastic Movement, supplied almost all of the education available to Europeans during the Middle Ages.

Scholasticism (the name comes from the scholars at the University of Paris) sought to reconcile the learning of Greece and Rome with that of the Christian world. Nothing would delight a Scholastic more than to find agreement and sympathy between the letters of ancient Greek philosopher Aristotle on one hand and church father St. Augustine (354–430) on the other. The Scholastic Movement, which began in Italy sometime in the twelfth century, had been full of vigor for some time. Its greatest mind had been St. Thomas Aquinas (1224–1274), who had made a masterful summary of the knowledge available to medieval humanity.

Had Erasmus lived even 200 years earlier, he would have thought the Scholastic Movement a great endeavor, but by the time he came to read its great books, they were outdated. The Latin in these books was obviously not the Latin of Rome, and the findings, whether scientific or theological, now seemed far off the mark. Things had become so tired and overdone that Scholastic disputations sometimes descended to a frivolous level, asking questions like "How many angels can dance on the head of a pin?"

Of all the faults of Scholasticism, it was the failure of its Latin that most angered Erasmus. He had, by about the age of 20, become a purist in linguistic matters. He wanted to trace the Latin of the Bible and other great works back to their classical sources and make sure that the meaning, as expressed by the original church fathers, was still acknowledged in his own time.

One might ask how one man presumed to find out so much where whole campuses and universities had failed. The answer is not complicated. Erasmus was a native genius, someone who took to scholarship the way another person might take to horseback riding or gymnastics. He saw quickly through the tired Latin of the Middle Ages and yearned for a return to the classical roots. Perhaps it was because he was not at a university and because he did so much reading on his own that he was able to see what many others did not. There had always been a place for the independent scholar within the Catholic Church; St. Thomas

Aquinas was the best example of this (to learn more about this philosopher, enter the keywords "Thomas Aquinas biography" into any Internet search engine and browse the listed sites). Erasmus, however, would eventually go beyond Aquinas and most of the other church fathers in his search for linguistic purity.

A more pressing problem was how Erasmus could advance in this quest while he was living at the monastery. The books there were old, and he had no access to original sources. Meanwhile, his commitment to the monastery was increasing. In the spring of 1492, the same year that Christopher Columbus crossed the Atlantic Ocean to the Americas, Erasmus took priestly vows.

Because of his pursuit of linguistic purity, Erasmus wanted to visit the great city of Rome. His fellow monks shared this

## HUMANISM

Humanism means, quite simply, an appreciation of human beings. During the long Middle Ages, most Christian Europeans had a negative opinion of humanity. They believed humans were weak, fallible, and vulnerable to temptation. The best a person could hope for was to escape from this life with his or her soul intact. Humanists, on the other hand, applauded the accomplishments of humans and believed that they were intrinsically worthy.

It is difficult to say exactly when humanistic movement began, but we can almost certainly say that it began in Italy. Italian poets like Petrarch (1304–1374) sang the praises of humanity, and wealthy Italians like the Medici banking family sponsored the sculptures of artists such as Donatello and Michelangelo. Two of the landmark moments in humanism were the unveiling of Donatello's bronze *David* in 1347 and the uncovering of Michelangelo's marble *David* in 1504, both in Florence, Italy.

Humanism gathered strength in the second half of the fifteenth century. Erasmus was aware of it through literary giants who came to the monastery to speak: One of these was the Dutchman Rudolph Agricola, who had gone to Italy to become steeped in the classics. From an early age, Erasmus had role models. His frustration was that he felt doomed to spend his time in a monastery that celebrated the traditions of the Middle Ages, rather than those of the new humanism.

desire; Rome was seen as the great destination for all Christian pilgrims. Most monks never saw Rome; they kept to their vows and remained within the monastery walls. There were some exceptions to the rule, and Erasmus took one of those rare opportunities.

Henry of Bergen, the bishop of Cambrai, aspired to the office of cardinal and intended to go to Rome to achieve this goal. The bishop needed a secretary, one who wrote well in Latin, and Erasmus was recommended to him. Sometime in 1495, Erasmus won a temporary assignment to the bishop's household, and he was able to leave the monastery for the first time in seven years.

Erasmus's friends were extremely envious of this opportunity. William Hermans, one of his friends from the monastery, wrote:

> I must stay and you will go
> To brave the Rhine and Alpine snow.
> To go for you, to stay for me,
> And you will see fair Italy.[15]

William Hermans and Erasmus remained friends long into the future, but Hermans surely learned that day (if he not known it before) that Erasmus's ambition took precedence over everything else. It was clear that his goal was to escape from the monastery and enter the open world once more.

# 3

# Paris and London

*"But you ask, 'How does our England please you?'* . . .
*I say I have never found a place I like so much."*

—Erasmus, in a letter from England

E rasmus celebrated his new freedom. The bishop of Cambrai was not a demanding taskmaster, and Erasmus was able to see little parts of the larger world. The dream of seeing Rome, however, was deferred, perhaps because the bishop lacked influence at the papal court.

Within a year of entering the bishop's service, Erasmus was anxious to be on the move again. He asked for, and received, the bishop's permission to study for a doctorate in theology. Because there was no suitable school close to hand, Erasmus was permitted to travel to Paris for his studies.

Paris. Even in the late fifteenth century, the word held a special charm. Paris was seen as the center of European intellectual life. This was the city of the theologian Abelard and Heloise, of the University of Paris and the Sorbonne. Unfortunately, it was also a city deeply divided.

The Hundred Years' War between France and England had been over for nearly 50 years, but the common people of Paris remembered that the faculty at the Sorbonne had supported the English—even against the French heroine Joan of Arc—in the great conflict. The faculty and students of the Sorbonne were bitterly contentious over the divide between humanism and Scholasticism.

### THE COLLEGE OF MONTAIGU

Erasmus enrolled at the College of Montaigu, part of the Sorbonne. To his terrible disappointment, he found that the college was run by a member of the old school who believed in putting the theological students through every kind of hardship and pain. No meat was allowed, and the only eggs that were served were rotten. Erasmus suffered horribly from the cold in the general dormitory and from the monotonous diet consisting of a lot of fish. Years later, in one of his *Colloquies*, he drew on his dull fish-eating days at the college when he wrote of the boredom in life:

**Butcher:** Say, you unsavory seller of salt fish, haven't you bought a rope yet?

**Fishmonger:** A rope, butcher?

**Butcher:** Yes, a rope.

**Fishmonger:** What for, in heaven's name?

**Butcher:** What for? To hang yourself with—what else?

**Fishmonger:** Others may buy them. I'm not yet so bored with life.

**Butcher:** But you soon *will* be bored with it.[16]

As bad as things were, Erasmus treasured his new freedom. He wandered the streets of Paris, found an occasional student to tutor, and generally considered the atmosphere much less oppressive than that of his native Holland. He had to send occasional letters to the bishop of Cambrai, assuring him that the doctorate in theology was progressing. Other than that, however, Erasmus was on his own.

Little is known of what Erasmus studied during these years. All his life, he tended to outrun disciplines. Where other students would read all the assigned material, Erasmus would go far beyond. Unlike most of his fellow students, he questioned the sources on which the material was based and made numerous notes for later critical inquiries.

With all of this activity one might wonder whether Erasmus ever rested. The answer is no—not in the usual sense of the word. Rest was less important to him than a good armchair in which he could read his newest book. Throughout his life, Erasmus displayed an extraordinary power of concentration. He was able to make notes while riding on horseback, he could study in the midst of a crowd, and he was seldom carried away by popular fancies. All of these traits combined to make him a formidable scholar.

It was during his time in Paris that Erasmus received one of his first opportunities to shine. He contacted the renowned humanist scholar Robert Gaugin. A doctor of theology and a consummate poet and essayist, Gaugin was known both for his impeccable scholarship and his rigorous honesty. Erasmus wrote a letter of self-introduction, and appears to have praised the great man too much. Gaugin wrote back:

> As Horace says, There does exist a Mean in all that is, and, in the end, appointed bounds are set. For this reason, Erasmus, I would wish that you had been more restrained in penning encomiums upon me, and had eschewed extravagance; not because praise makes me blush, but because, whenever undeserved plaudits are awarded by a speaker they are put down to flattery or falsehood. I shall therefore write frankly. So far as I can tell by your letter and your lyric poems, I judge you to be a scholar.[17]

From Gaugin, this was high praise indeed. Just a few months later, Gaugin would have his *Compendium of the Deeds of the French* printed. Gaugin fell ill as the task was near completion, and the printer informed him that two folio pages were unfilled. This had to be rectified, and Gaugin asked Erasmus to do him the honor of writing a letter that would fill out the book. Erasmus complied and did so with such a flourish that his name was now heard for the first time in major literary circles.

Erasmus was delighted with this turn of events, but he lived in constant fear that the bishop of Cambrai would summon him back to Holland or that the monastery at Steyn would recall him. Erasmus therefore wrote long letters of flattery both to the bishop and the abbot, assuring them that he was coming along in his studies and would one day reward them with a doctorate in theology. As time passed, both the bishop and the abbot became suspicious. How was it that a man like Erasmus, so gifted with his tongue and his pen, should take such a long time to earn his degree?

### TRAVEL TO ENGLAND

In 1497 or 1498, Erasmus struck up a friendship with an English nobleman. William Blount, Lord Mountjoy, was in Paris for a number of reasons, but his main purpose was to work on improving his classical knowledge. He hired Erasmus as his tutor, and the two became fast friends. When Lord Mountjoy returned to England in 1499, Erasmus went with him as a guest.

England in 1499 was a land of about three million people. It was less populated than its Continental neighbors and was considered by many Europeans a less civilized nation. Erasmus put this allegation to the test and decided the opposite. One of his first letters was written to John Fisher, an Englishman who happened to be in Rome while Erasmus was in London:

> I too have made some progress in England. The Erasmus you knew has already become quite a respectable sportsman; he is not a bad horseman either, and quite a skilful [sic] courtier, for he is distinctly mannerly in his salutations and concilia-tory in address; and in all this, quite at variance with his own temperament. But what do I care? for it suits me very well. Do please come over here quickly yourself. Why are you so complacently burying your wit among French dunghills while you turn into an old man . . . if you were fully aware of what England has to offer, you would rush hither.[18]

Erasmus went on to commend the English for their manners:

> There is, besides, one custom which can never be commended too highly. When you arrive anywhere, you are received with kisses on all sides, and when you take your leave they speed you on your way with kisses. The kisses are renewed when you come back. . . . In a word, wherever you turn, the world is full of kisses.[19]

Ironically, this multiple kissing was actually a French custom that had been brought to the English court during the rule of the Plantagenet kings (1154–1399). The reason Erasmus had not encountered it in France was that he had consorted with the clergy rather than the nobility.

Historians do not know the actual day that Erasmus first met Thomas More, and this is a significant gap in historical knowledge because this was the beginning of one of the greatest friendships in literary history. Writers and poets are often jealous of each other, both of their works and their affections, and it is rare indeed that two extraordinary writers can also be great friends. This was the case, however, between Erasmus and Thomas More.

## JOHN COLET

Born in London in 1474, John Colet was the son of a man who had twice been Lord Mayor of London. Colet grew up in prosperous circumstances, but by a terrible stroke of bad fortune, he was one of only two children to survive out of a family of twenty-two children! These early losses no doubt contributed to making him a pious, severe, and occasionally gloomy man.

Colet spent several years on the Continent during the 1490s. He absorbed a good deal of the new humanism and, when he returned to England, he became one of the leaders of that movement. Thomas Linacre, Thomas More, and John Colet were the backbone of what is considered the early humanistic movement in England.

Colet inherited his father's fortune in 1509 and set about at once to create the new St. Paul's School. Located in the churchyard of St. Paul's Cathedral, the new school emphasized both the ancient masters and the new humanistic learning. Colet kept the number of boys (who paid no tuition) to a limit of 153 (the number was selected as being one of biblical significance).

The boys who graduated from St. Paul's became the deans, rectors, and priests who brought the new humanism to English churches. Many of them later participated in the English Reformation movement, which began when King Henry VIII broke from the Catholic Church in Rome in order to grant himself a divorce from his queen.

Colet died in 1519. On learning the news, Erasmus wrote that the death pierced his heart, so dear had Colet's love of learning been to him.

More was about 12 years younger than Erasmus. Born into moderate wealth, More had never had to endure anything like the struggles of Erasmus. In most circumstances, this difference would have made Erasmus very envious, but he made an exception in More's case. One of Erasmus's letters, written from London, described the small circle of philosophers that included More:

> But you ask, "How does our England please you?" If you trust me at all, dear Robert, I should wish you to trust me when I say that I have never found a place I like so much. I find here a climate at once agreeable and extremely healthy and such a quantity of intellectual refinement and scholarship, not of the usual pedantic and trivial kind either, but profound and learned and truly classical, in both Latin and Greek, that I have little longing left for Italy, except for the sake of visiting it. . . . Did Nature ever create anything kinder, sweeter, or more harmonious than the character of Thomas More? [20]

For the first time in his life, Erasmus was in the company of other humanists like himself. They were sincere men of the Church, but they also venerated the classical tradition of ancient Greece and Rome. If these two noble strains could be joined together—if the Christian and the classical could truly unite— then the world would be a glorious place indeed! This was the hope of men like Erasmus and Thomas More.

The only thing that might have imperiled Erasmus's new friendship with Thomas More was a social gaffe. More took Erasmus to the apartments of the royal family on an impromptu visit. The king and queen were not there, but the three royal children were present. Erasmus was deeply impressed with the nine-year-old Prince Henry, who would later become King Henry VIII. When the child asked for a present, More had a verse ready; Erasmus had nothing in hand. Erasmus was mortified as he and More rode away. He swiftly composed a poem likening Prince Henry to his father, King Henry VII, and had it sent to the palace.

The episode did not harm the affection between Erasmus and the prince, which continued for many years. Erasmus would have broken off his relationship with many other friends had they allowed him to face such an embarrassing moment, but Erasmus forgave More.

Sadly, Erasmus did not remain in England for long. By the middle of 1500, he was eager to travel to a new destination. He bade farewell to his many English friends and headed for the coast with 20 pounds sterling in his pocket. This was the greatest sum that Erasmus had yet amassed in life. Unfortunately, he was deprived of 18 pounds of it by the customs inspectors at Dover. King Henry VII had laid down a strict law forbidding the exportation of English currency.

As he sailed from Dover to Calais, France, Erasmus looked back with a mixture of wonder and regret. Never before had he met so many persons of intellectual distinction and good will. Historians continue to wonder why he decided to leave.

# 4

# Venice
# and Rome

*"Do not let your relationship with God depend on food,
on a particular form of worship, or on any visible
thing. . . . Whatever things you find Christ's image in,
join yourself to them."*

—Erasmus, *Handbook
of the Militant Christian*

By the end of 1500, Erasmus was back in Paris. His letters made little mention of the turn of the century or of any impending great changes that the new age might bring. As usual, Erasmus was most interested in his literary endeavors, and he had made great progress on one of his first: his *Adages*.

Adages (the word was coined by Erasmus himself) are much like proverbs. Proverbial knowledge or wisdom is that which one gathers through conversations with all sorts of people (to learn more about these sayings, enter the keywords "common proverbs" into any Internet search engine and browse the listed sites). We tend to think of Erasmus as consorting only with churchmen or nobility, but he had an unusually strong need for conversation, so a ploughman or carriage driver would do well if there was no one else available. From these people, Erasmus picked up the bits and pieces that became his *Adages*, first published in Paris in 1500 (they were revised and reprinted many times afterward).

*Adages* was full of sayings that still resonate with the modern mind: expressions like "the grass is greener in the next field" and "one hand washes the other." Erasmus enlivened his adages with commentaries in Latin. He tried to make the most of commonplace knowledge. Because he put it all in elegant Latin text, his work was read by scholars and by the general reading public. *Adages* was not a true best-seller, but it contributed mightily to Erasmus's reputation. He had come a long way in the decade since he had been ordained a priest at the monastery.

The monastery at Steyn was rightly suspicious of this runaway monk and priest even though Erasmus continued to send half-hearted letters both to the monastery and to the bishop of Cambrai, insisting that he was indeed still working on his doctorate in theology. In truth, Erasmus now gave himself over wholeheartedly to writing popular but elegant works for the public. He began to realize that he might "make it" as a man of letters.

The bishop of Cambrai, not surprisingly, cut Erasmus off without any further subsidies. By then, Erasmus had found something of a second patron in a widowed noblewoman named Ann de Vere. Her castle at Tournehem in Belgium was always open to him, and she sometimes sent him small sums of money. Overall, however, Erasmus continued to struggle financially. Despite his own hardships, he was generous to others. Younger scholars could find no better or friendlier patron than Erasmus, but he sometimes became bitter to see that he was still struggling to survive on workman's wages.

## HANDBOOK OF THE MILITANT CHRISTIAN

In 1503, Erasmus's *Handbook of the Militant Christian* (*Enchiridion Militis Christiani*) was published in Paris. This turned out to be his greatest early success. Erasmus always claimed that the book was written as a guide for the husband of one of his female friends. The wife was a devout Christian; her husband was not. Therefore, she asked Erasmus to describe the actions and thoughts proper to a good Christian, so that she might give her husband a model of behavior. Erasmus agreed, and the start of the book sounded his theme of eternal caution:

> In this life it is necessary that we be on our guard. To begin with we must be constantly aware of the fact that life here below is best described as being a type of continual warfare. This is a fact that Job [in the Old Testament], that undefeated soldier of vast experience, tells us so plainly. Yet in this matter the great majority of mankind is often deceived, for the world, like some deceitful magician, captivates their minds with seductive blandishments, and as a result most individuals behave as if there had been a cessation of hostilities. They celebrate as if they were assured of victory when, as a matter of fact, genuine peace could never be further away.[21]

Did Erasmus mean violent warfare, such as that between the Christians and the Ottoman Turks? No, he meant the subtle, insidious invasions of Satan, which catch people off-guard and lead them into temptation. Erasmus, still speaking to the husband, continued:

> To return to our original purpose. We must forge a handy weapon, an enchiridion, a dagger, that you can always carry

with you. You must be on guard when you eat or sleep, even when you travel in the course of worldly concerns and perhaps become weary of bearing this righteous armor. Never allow yourself to become totally disarmed, even for a moment, lest your wily foe oppress you. Do not be ashamed to carry this little sword with you. For it is neither a hardship to bear, nor useless in defending yourself. Though it is a small weapon, it will enable you, if you use it skillfully, to withstand the enemy's tumultuous assaults quite easily and avoid a deadly wound. Now is the time for us to teach ourselves a kind of "manual of arms."[22]

There followed a long stream of evils that the good Christian should combat. Foremost among them were lust, avarice, ambition, pride and haughtiness, and anger and revenge. Erasmus's cure for each of these great troubles was for the good Christian to find a middle way between temptation and the consolations of heaven. If he could, Erasmus would have his good Christian resist all temptations, and he held out the promise that the way became easier the more it was practiced. In his conclusion, Erasmus urged a quiet attention to the Bible:

> Monasticism is not holiness, but a kind of life that can be useful or useless depending on a person's temperament and disposition. I neither recommend it nor do I condemn it. Let me warn you about it, however. Do not let your relationship with God depend on food, on a particular form of worship, or on any visible thing, but only on those things we have already gone over. Whatever things you find Christ's image in, join yourself to them. If people do not think along lines that would make you better, withdraw yourself as much as possible from human companionship and take for companions Christ and His prophets and Apostles.[23]

It has often been said that "we teach the things we need to learn," and this seems to be true in the case of Erasmus. When he urged his readers to withdraw from human companionship, he overlooked the fact that this was almost impossible for him to do himself. Erasmus always craved good company.

*Handbook of the Militant Christian* was a major success. Erasmus was now a leading member of the Parisian literary establishment. His success brought him many admirers, but he had almost as many foes, people who were envious of his accomplishments. Then, in 1506, came the opportunity for which he had waited so long: a chance to see Italy.

## WORK IN ITALY

Erasmus went to England for a short visit. There, he met King Henry VII's physician, Boerio, who had two sons he wanted to send to Italy for their education. Boerio asked if Erasmus would consent to be their intellectual guardian for the journey. Erasmus could not have asked for a better assignment.

Erasmus and his young charges set out from Paris in August. The little party crossed the Alps and reached Turin where Erasmus, somewhat to his surprise, was awarded his doctorate in theology from the university there. Turin may have been delighted to be the first to offer such a distinction to the man who was becoming known as the greatest scholar of his generation. For his part, Erasmus was pleased to finally have the doctorate, but he made rather little of it. He had already come to recognize that the works of his own pen were more valuable to him than the degrees of any school.

The party pushed on to Bologna where Erasmus was shocked to see the army of Pope Julius II enter the city. Julius was the most materialistic and ambitious of all the Renaissance era popes, the only one to actually don armor and go forth into combat. Erasmus was deeply offended by this display of worldly power from the Holy See. Years later, he penned the rather vicious "Julius Exclusus," describing how St. Peter greeted Julius at the gates of heaven:

> **Julius:** What the devil is up? The gates not open? Some one has monkied with the lock.
>
> **Peter:** Maybe you have the wrong key. You've got the key of power.

**Julius:** It's the only one I ever had. I'll bang. Hey, porter, are you asleep or drunk?

**Peter:** Immortal God, what a stench! I'll peek through this crack till I know what's up. Who are you?

**Julius:** Can't you seek this key, the triple crown, and the pallium sparkling with gems.

**Peter:** It doesn't look like the key Christ gave me. How should I know the crown which no barbarian tyrant ever dared to wear. As for the gems and the jewels I trample them under my feet.

**Julius:** Come on now. I am Julius the Ligurian and I suppose you know these two letters (pointing to his chest) P. M., if you can read.

**Peter:** Pestis Maxima.

**Julius:** Pontifex Maximus.

**Peter:** I don't care if you're Mercury Trismegistus, unless your life is saintly.[24]

Needless to say, Julius was refused admittance to heaven in this satire. It was written around 1517, more than ten years after Erasmus had seen Pope Julius in Bologna.

Erasmus found Rome something of a disappointment. There were scholars and manuscripts to be sure, but he found less enthusiasm for what he considered the true humanities than he had in England. Erasmus was almost ready to abandon his entire Italian visit when a letter came to him from Aldus Manutius, the greatest printer and publisher of the age (printing and publishing were performed by the same institution, or "house," in those days).

A native of the Italian island of Capri, Manutius now lived in Venice. For some years, he had been reprinting classical studies in Latin. Manutius was the first printer or publisher to use italic letters; he found that using italics allowed him to place more letters and words on each page, making it cheaper to mass-produce his books. Manutius, however, was no mere reproducer. He was a man with serious scholarly interests who took great care in his selection of authors and texts, and he worked carefully to turn out beautiful works of art. Erasmus was thrilled to be invited to Venice by such a man.

A charming story is often told of Erasmus's arrival in Venice. Aldus Manutius was busy that day, as indeed he was every day. Because Erasmus arrived alone and was not well dressed, Manutius kept him waiting for some time, thinking that this was a person of no great importance. When he discovered his error, Manutius not only made Erasmus profusely welcome but invited him to live in his own household.

Manutius was every inch the printer and publisher that Erasmus had hoped. The two of them worked closely together on a new

## THE HOUSE OF MANUTIUS

Aldus Manutius began printing in the 1490s. By that time, there was already a strong printing tradition in northern Italy. The sisters of a Dominican convent in Florence had printed numerous works from ancient Rome. Manutius, however, was the one who made Italian printing preeminent in his time.

Starting around 1500, Manutius pioneered in the use of italic letters. The primary reason for this was that he could fit more characters (letters) on the printed page with italic type. He also found that the italics could make the page more attractive and thereby attract more book buyers.

Manutius had a thriving establishment when Erasmus arrived in 1508. A number of itinerant scholars lived in the home of Manutius's uncle, forming a scholarly community. One of these men was Jerome Aleander, an Italian humanist. He and Erasmus became good friends during their days in Venice, but later became bitter enemies after the Reformation began.

Erasmus left the House of Manutius sometime in 1508, never to return. At a number of times in later life, he would sigh and regret having left, since he had seldom found such a congenial group of scholars elsewhere.

Manutius continued to print until his death in 1515. He was one of the first truly international printers and he showed that printing could be both honorable and profitable.

edition of the *Adages*. The number of proverbs was expanded from 838 in the 1500 edition to 3,260 in the 1508 edition. The Greek sources were much more clearly explicated in this new version, and Erasmus was well pleased with the result. At Manutius's house, Erasmus, like everyone else, worked at breakneck speed. He later complained that he did not have the time to scratch his ears. Despite his complaints, the results were wonderful.

Erasmus also took the time to bring out a new publication, his *Dulce bellum inexpertis* ("Sweet is war to him who has had no taste of it"). Erasmus had long been a pacifist at heart, but he now made this belief an outward and obvious one. He ridiculed the old men who chose to send young men off to wars, and he lamented that Christians should fight against one another. Rather than call for a general Christian crusade against the Ottoman Turks, Erasmus called for education that would bring the Turks to Christianity of their own will.

The only major problem of the Venetian stay was food. Erasmus had always suffered from both a light head and a weak stomach. Breakfast was not served until 10:00 A.M. and dinner was very late. Erasmus endured this regimen for a year and a half, both because of Manutius's expertise and because of the good company he found at the house. Erasmus finally left Venice and made his way to Florence. He felt he had stayed too long in Italy and was eager to return to northern Europe, but he also wondered what city or university would accept him. In answer to his wondering about his future came the welcome letter from William Blount, Lord Mountjoy. Reminding Erasmus of his earlier love of England and of his friendship with young Prince Henry, Lord Mountjoy pointed out that Prince Henry had become King Henry VIII. Surely scholarship would prosper in England. He urged Erasmus to come.

Erasmus went. In the spring of 1510, with pen in hand, Erasmus rode north over the Alps, making sketches and notes for what would become his most famous work and the greatest best-seller of the entire Renaissance era.

# 5

# The Praise of Folly

*"Folly is the best preservative of youth, and the most effectual antidote against any age . . . "*

—Erasmus, *The Praise of Folly*

*T*he *Praise of Folly* is one of the most widely read books of all human history. What is most remarkable is that no two readers seem to have exactly the same reaction to the book. Some find it satirical; others find it bitter; still others feel that it evokes a profound, though disguised, Christian faith. This is no average book, but it is one for all ages and seasons. Erasmus dedicated the work to his beloved friend Thomas More:

> I resolved to make some sport with the praise of folly. But who the devil put that in your head? you'll say. The first thing was your surname of More, which comes so near the word *Moriae* (folly) as you are far from the thing. And that you are so, all the world will clear you. In the next place, I conceived this exercise of wit would not be least approved by you; inasmuch as you are wont to be delighted with such kind of mirth, that is to say, neither unlearned, if I am not mistaken, nor altogether insipid, and in the whole course of your life have played the part of a Democritus.[25]

To liken More's name to folly may seem a backhanded compliment. Another sort of man might have been put off by the comparison, but Thomas More loved it. He became one of the greatest admirers of Erasmus's book.

The book begins with Erasmus taking on the voice of Folly. She is a woman, dressed in cap and bells to signify her foolishness. She begins:

> How slightly soever I am esteemed in the common vogue of the world (for I know how disingenuously Folly is decried, even by those who are themselves the greatest fools) yet it is from my influence alone that the whole universe receives her ferment of mirth and jollity.[26]

Folly goes on to explain that the world would not turn, people would not marry, and there would be no future generations of humans were it not for her gift to the world. Who would be so rash as to marry if he knew what it might entail, and who would ever allow herself to become pregnant if she could foretell the arduous work ahead? Only Folly allows humans to overcome their objections and forge ahead. Folly then describes her ancestry and lineage:

> First then, my father was neither the chaos, nor hell, nor Saturn, nor Jupiter, nor any of those old worn out, grandsire gods, but Plutus, the very same that, maugre Homer, Hesiod, nay, in spite of Jove himself, was the primary father of the universe, at whose beck alone, for all ages religion and civil policy have been successively undermined and re-established— by whose powerful influence war, peace, empire, debates, justice, magistracy, marriage, leagues, compacts, laws, arts (I have almost run out of breath) but in a word, all affairs of church and state, and business of private concern, are severally ordered and administered.[27]

What are we to make of this run-on sentence? Part of the trouble is that Erasmus's Latin tended to run on far more than does our modern-day English, but is also true that Erasmus intended to confound the readers of his time as well as future readers. Erasmus did not wish to be easily understood; he was, after all, promoting the cause of Folly over good sense or even sanity. To extend his point, Erasmus quoted from the Greek playwright Sophocles: "To know nothing is the sweetest life."[28]

## FOLLY'S MOCKERY

Erasmus poked fun at the people among whom he had grown up. Holland is a target; youth and old age are also mocked:

> Folly is the best preservative of youth, and the most effectual antidote against age, and it is a never-failing observation made of the people of Brabant, that, contrary to the proverb of older and wiser, the more ancient they grow, the more foolish they are; and there is no any one country, whose inhabitants enjoy themselves better, and rub throughout the world with more ease and quiet. To these are related, as well by affinity of customs as by neighborhood, my friends, the

Hollanders. Mine, I may well call them, for they stick so close and lovingly to me, that they are styled fools to a proverb, and yet scorn to be ashamed of the name.[29]

Indeed, no one was safe from Folly (or Erasmus). He goes on to mock both friendship and marriage:

Good God! What frequent divorces or worse mischief would oft sadly happen, were it not that man and wife were so discreet as to pass over light occasions of quarrel with laughing, jesting, dissembling, and such like playing the fool? Nay, how few matches would go forward, if the hasty lover did but first know how many little tricks of lust and wantonness (and perhaps more gross failings) his coy and seemingly bashful mistress had oft been guilty of? And how few marriages, when consummated, would continue happy, if the husband were not either sottishly insensible of, or did not purposely wink at and pass over the lightness and forwardness of his good-natured wife? This peace and quiet is owing to my management, for there would otherwise be continual jars and broils, and mad doings, if want of wit only did not at the same time make a contented cuckold and a still house.[30]

Erasmus went on to deride the thoughts of the greatest Greek philosophers. If Socrates and Plato were so wise, why did the former commit suicide and the latter fall into silly daydreams about an idyllic social republic? Did they not know better?

How! you will say, this is absurd and contradictory; the east and west may as soon shake hands as Folly and Wisdom be reconciled. Well, but have a little patience and I will warrant you I will make out my claim. First then, if wisdom (as must be confessed) is no more than a readiness of doing good, and an expeditious method of becoming serviceable to the world, to whom does this virtue more properly belong? To the wise man, who partly out of modesty, partly out of cowardice, can proceed resolutely in no attempt; or to the fool, that goes hand over head, leaps before he looks, and so ventures through the most hazardous undertaking without any sense or prospect of danger?[31]

Erasmus also had some choice words for those who believed in indulgences and other certificates or merit from the Catholic Church. Bear in mind that he wrote *The Praise of Folly* in 1511,

## THE SHIP OF FOOLS

Erasmus was a profoundly original writer, but he sometimes built on the thoughts of others. This was true to some extent in *The Praise of Folly*, for Erasmus, like every other educated European, had read Sebastian Brant's *The Ship of Fools*, first published in 1494.

Brant's book was well known to generation after generation of Europeans, but it has seldom been translated into English. One of the first, and best, attempts at translation was made by Edwin Zaydel, published in 1944. Zaydel put Sebastian Brant's words into rhyming couplets, one example of which is his "Fools now as before":

> A fool who hears what wise men say
>
> But never profits day by day,
>
> Who wants to hear what would behoove
>
> But never wisely would improve.
>
> He wants to own whate'er he spies
>
> And shows all men he's far from wise,
>
> For every fool this flaw doth show:
>
> What's new, for that he'd crave and glow,
>
> But soon of novelty they tire
>
> And other novelty desire.*

Brant's book was in many ways a precursor to Erasmus's *The Praise of Folly*. When the two men met at Strasbourg in 1514, Brant hailed Erasmus. They recognized each other as kindred spirits.

* Edwin H. Zaydel, *The Ship of Fools by Sebastian Brant, Translated into Rhyming Couplets.* (New York: Dover Publications, 1944), pp. 140–141.

DESIDERIUS
ERASMUS

With permission from the bishop of Cambrai, Erasmus attended the Sorbonne, the famous university in Paris, to earn his doctorate in theology. Though Erasmus found the food bland and dormitories a bit stark, the atmosphere of the university was generally less oppressive than what he had known at the monastery at Steyn, and Erasmus felt no urgency to return. It would take him almost a decade to receive his degree.

Erasmus met Thomas More during his first trip to England in 1499. The meeting of the two intellectuals soon resulted in a great friendship that would last their entire lives. More, a devout Catholic, wrote many works, but his most famous is *Utopia*, a novel describing an ideal society in which each individual strived for knowledge and followed the religion of his choice. More was beheaded for his refusal to recognize King Henry VIII as the head of the church, rather than the pope, in 1535.

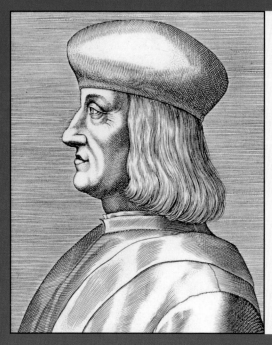

Aldus Manutius is generally considered the greatest printer of his time. Manutius was the first to use italic letters, which allowed him to fit more letters on the page. He set up shop in Venice, where he worked with Erasmus on his *Adages*. It was while collaborating with Manutius that Erasmus expanded *Adages* from a book of 838 proverbs into one of over three thousand.

Pope Leo X was delighted by the three-page dedication Erasmus cunningly included in his translation of the Bible, *Novum Instrumentum*. Erasmus's flattery paid off a year later when the pope absolved Erasmus of any penalties he might have received for deserting the monastic life. It was under Pope Leo X's rule that the Roman Catholic Church authorized the sale of indulgences to fund the construction of St. Peter's Basilica.

Martin Luther was an Augustinian monk and priest who became disgusted with the church's sale of indulgences in order to finance the construction of St. Peter's Basilica in Rome. Hoping to incite church reform, Luther wrote a document now known as the Ninety-Five Theses, which included arguments against indulgences. He reportedly nailed the document to the church door in Wittenburg, Germany, in 1517, causing a great uproar within the church. Although Erasmus was asked to take sides in the matter, he would not commit to either cause.

King Henry VIII of England and King Francis I of France, depicted in the top left of this illustration, met in Belgium at a place so beautiful it became known as the Field of the Cloth of Gold. Though the two leaders met to negotiate their own alliances, Erasmus traveled to the summit to persuade Henry VIII to help Martin Luther, whose protests against the church put him in a dangerous position. Henry VIII refused to offer Luther his protection.

Erasmus spent 1516–1517 in Basel, Switzerland, working with the printer John Froben on his latest work, *Novum Instrumentum* (the New Testament), which garnered much praise. Erasmus returned in 1521 and stayed for eight years, the closest thing he ever had to a permanent residence.

The Peasants' Rebellion broke out in Germany in 1524, resulting in the death of about 100,000 people. The peasants, who were born basically without freedom in a condition known as serfdom, were inspired to revolt by Martin Luther's concept of the freedom of the Christian man. Rather than supporting the peasants, Luther wrote essays to the German nobles encouraging them to strike back at the rebels.

fully six years before Martin Luther penned his mighty attack on the sale of indulgences:

> What shall I say of such as cry up and maintain the cheat of pardons and indulgences? That by these compute the time of each soul's residence in purgatory, and assign them a longer or shorter continuance, according as they purchase more or fewer of these paltry pardons, and saleable exemptions? Or what can be said bad enough about others, who pretend that by the force of such magical charms, or by the fumbling over their beads in the rehearsal of such and such petitions (which some religious impostors invented, either for diversion, or what is more likely, for advantage) they shall procure riches, honor, pleasure, health, long life, a lusty old age, nay, after death a sitting at the right hand of our Savior?[32]

All his life, Erasmus had been a cosmopolitan, an international Christian rather than a Dutchman, a Frenchman, an Englishman, or an Italian (each one of these nations could at least claim he had lived there). Sparing none, Erasmus (Folly) saved some of his witticisms to describe the absurdity of nationalism:

> Upon this account it is that the English challenge the prerogative of having the most handsome women, of being the most accomplished in the science of music, and of keeping the best tables. The Scotch brag of their gentility, and pretend the genius of their native soil inclines them to be good disputants. The French think themselves remarkable for complaisance and good breeding; the Sorbonists of Paris pretend before any others to have made the greatest proficiency in polemic divinity. The Italians value themselves for learning and eloquence: and, like the Grecians of old, account all the world barbarians compared to themselves; to which piece of vanity the inhabitants of Rome are more especially addicted, pretending themselves to be owners of all those heroic virtues, which their city so many ages since was deservedly famous for. The Venetians stand upon their birth and pedigree. The Grecians pride themselves in having been the first

inventors of most arts, and in their country being famed for the product of so many eminent philosophers. The Turks, and all the other refuse of Mahometanism, pretend they profess the only true religion, and laugh at all Christians for superstitious, narrow-souled fools. The Jews to this day expect their Messiah as devoutly as they believe in their first prophet Moses. The Spaniards challenge the repute of being accounted good soldiers. And the Germans are noted for their tall, proper stature, and for their skill in magic.[33]

Had Folly (Erasmus) left anyone out? To ensure that no one had been excluded, Erasmus next turned to philosophers and authors:

Of the same gang are those scribbling fops, who think to eternalize their memory by setting up for authors: among which, though they are all in some way indebted to me, yet are those more especially so, who spoil paper in blotting it with mere trifles and impertinences. For as to those graver drudgers to the press, that write learnedly, beyond the reach of an ordinary reader, who dare submit their labors to the review of the most severe critics, these are not so liable to be envied for their honor, as to be pitied for their toil and slavery.[34]

Here, Erasmus spoke from experience. He had labored long in the literary vineyards and knew how slender were the rewards:

They make additions, alterations, blot out, write anew, amend, interline, turn it upside down, and yet can never please their fickle judgment, but that they shall dislike the next hour what they penned in the former; and all this to purchase the airy commendations of a few critical readers, which at most is but a poor reward for all their fastings, watchings, confinements, and brain-breaking tortures of invention.[35]

## DEFENSE OF CHRISTIANITY

Having mocked marriage, friendship, scholarship, indulgences, and nationalism, Folly changes her tone. The change is subtle but profound. In the last 30 pages or so, *The Praise of Folly* takes on a quiet, subdued, but unmistakable defense of the Christian faith. To begin, Folly praises St. Paul: "Nay, St. Paul himself, that great doctor of the Gentiles, writing to his Corinthians, readily owns the name, saying, *If any man speak as a fool, I am more*; as if to have been less so had been a reproach and a disgrace." [36] A bit farther on, he wrote:

> Thus indeed St. Paul himself minces and mangles some citations he makes use of, and seems to wrest them to a different sense from that for which they were first intended, as is confessed by the great linguist, St. Hierom. Thus, when that apostle saw at Athens the inscription of an altar, he draws from it an argument for the proof of the Christian religion; but leaving out a great part of the sentence, which perhaps if fully recited might have prejudiced his cause, he mentions only the two last words, viz., To the unknown God; and this too not without alteration, for the whole inscription ran thus: To the Gods of Asia, Europe, and Africa, to all foreign and unknown Gods. [37]

Folly (Erasmus) then turned to Jesus himself to make her point:

> To the same purpose did our blessed Lord frequently condemn and upbraid the scribes, Pharisees, and lawyers, while he carries himself kind and obliging to the unlearned multitude: For what otherwise can be the meaning of that tart denunciation, Woe unto you, scribes and Pharisees, than woe unto you wise men, whereas he seems chiefly delighted with children, women, and illiterate fishermen. We may farther take notice, that among all the several kinds of brute creatures he shows greatest liking to such as are farthest distant from the subtlety of the fox. Thus in his progress to Jerusalem he chose to ride sitting upon an ass, though, if he pleased, he might have mounted the back of a lion with more of state, and as little of danger. The Holy Spirit chose rather likewise to descend from heaven in the shape of a simple guileless dove, than that of an eagle, kite, or other more lofty fowl. [38]

*The Praise of Folly* moves to its end. In the final scene, Folly assumes her mocking manner once more, but the discerning reader is not deceived. Erasmus has done a masterful job of cloaking his Christian piety in the guise of mockery. If he is a fool, and if Folly is everywhere to be seen, then it is a Folly that guides men and women to a Christian destiny.

# The Wheel of Fortune

"*My mind was attracted solely to literature, which is not practiced in [the monastic community]. In fact I feel certain that, had I entered upon some free kind of life, I could have been accounted good as well as happy.*"

—Erasmus, in a letter describing his aversion to the monastic life

Life was never quite the same again for Erasmus. He reached a new peak of popularity and acclaim with *The Praise of Folly*, and his name became a household word. The book was reprinted three times in the year 1512 alone.

By then, Erasmus was at Cambridge University in England. He generally preferred the "town" to the "gown," and London had always been his favorite English haunt, but some things had changed. Thomas More had married a second time, and his new wife was not nearly as receptive to guests as the first had been. Erasmus therefore went to Cambridge where, for the first time in his life, he had something of a regular job and a regular income.

Alas, Erasmus found, as many people do, that expenses rise just as quickly as incomes. One calculation has it that Erasmus was earning close to 95 pounds a year at this time (recall that 20 pounds had been a fortune to him in 1500) but his expenses had risen to about 120 pounds per year. As usual, Erasmus had to pack in more work than other people would consider possible. He translated several works from Greek to Latin, taught a few courses at Cambridge, and kept up with his ever-increasing correspondence. His fame brought him letters from far and wide, and he did his very best to answer them all.

While at Cambridge, Erasmus developed a correspondence with Andrea Ammonio. The Italian was a representative of Pope Julius II, but he and Erasmus delighted in poking fun both at international politics and at the peculiar habits of the English people. In November 1511, Ammonio wrote:

> Either my servant is exceptionally unlucky, so that all he does for me turns out badly, or else the Cambridge rabble surpasses even the rest of the disobliging British nation in incivility, so unaware is it of all obligations and so devoid of absolutely every kind of civilized behavior. I long to see a few of this sort measure their length on a gallows! Why, they have practically no idea what it means to take responsibility for a letter, and fail to deliver it afterwards; to put it in the mildest way possible,

they do not know how many people they are cheating of the pleasure that should be theirs, or how many good men's good name for conscientiousness they may be ruining. . . . Oh these savages! I swear I'd gladly see them torn to pieces any day![39]

These were not by any means the only troubles. Both Ammonio and Erasmus were disturbed by the recent revival of warfare in their neighborhood. In 1511, Pope Julius II continued his war against France; Julius arranged a Holy Alliance among Rome, Venice, and England, all of which were to carry out the war. Although Erasmus had lived in France in earlier years, his loyalties were certainly divided: he had also lived, however briefly, in Rome, Venice, and now England. More importantly, he was at heart a pacifist, and he deplored the apparent trend toward violence.

The plague was abroad as well. Erasmus narrowly missed death from the sweating sickness in 1511, and he was lucky to escape the plague that same year (to learn more about this disease, enter the keywords "bubonic plague Europe" into any Internet search engine and browse the listed sites). However fragile his constitution was, he had a remarkable tendency either to escape disease or survive it. He counted himself lucky to be alive and reckoned that many of his contemporaries had not achieved his age.

Cambridge University was not the ideal place for Erasmus. The school had lagged behind Oxford University for some time, and there was still no printing press at Cambridge. But one thing the place did have was a treasure trove of Greek manuscripts, and Erasmus made the most of this opportunity. He had long been convinced that three great languages were needed for an understanding of scripture: Latin, Greek, and Hebrew. He was a master at the first and was making good progress in the second, but he would eventually abandon any hope of learning the last.

At the same time, Erasmus was in the midst of developing his greatest scholarly work. He had been interested in the early fathers of the Christian Church for nearly 20 years and had now fastened upon St. Jerome and the Vulgate edition of the Bible for his study. Erasmus was certainly not the only person of his time to pursue this interest, but he was the only one who intended to follow the interest both in Latin and in Greek. He wrote to John Colet: "I have finished the collation of the New Testament and am now starting on St. Jerome. After this is done, back I fly to you and yours."[40]

### REJECTING THE MONASTIC LIFE

As was often the case, Erasmus deceived himself. He was not to "fly" back to John Colet or any other English scholars. He was too "fiddle-footed" to stay in any one place for long.

Erasmus returned to Holland for a brief visit in 1514. Around this time, he received a letter from one of his oldest friends, Servatius Rogers, who had since become the abbot of the monastery at Steyn. It was to Servatius that Erasmus had written his youthful letters full of love that led the friendship to end. Servatius's letter has not survived, but Erasmus's reply remains intact. Erasmus left no doubt as to his life choices: "Most gracious Father, after a stormy passage through many hands, your letter finally reached me, but only after I had left England. It has given me infinite pleasure, redolent as it is of your feelings towards me in the past."[41] In the letter, Erasmus described how ill suited he was to the monastic life:

> I was clearly conscious how ill adapted I was to the life, for not everything suits everyone. Through some peculiarity of my constitution I have always found it hard to endure fasting. Once I was awakened I never could go to sleep again for several hours. My mind was attracted solely to literature, which is not practiced in your community. In fact I feel certain that, had I entered upon some free kind of life, I could have been accounted good as well as happy.[42]

Some of the points Erasmus made seem rather silly. Is not everyone's constitution ill adapted to fasting? Surely, there was some type of literature at the monastery at Steyn—just not the type that Erasmus admired. Besides, Erasmus overlooked the key point. He had entered the monastery of his own free will and we can logically question what right he had to cast away his vows. He continued with a somewhat skewed interpretation of those times:

> I decided to bear with courage this part of my unhappiness also. For you know that I have been unfortunate in many respects. But I have always regarded as the worst of my misfortunes the fact that I had been forced into the kind of profession which was utterly repugnant to my mind and body alike.[43]

Now, after many years in London, Paris, Venice, and elsewhere, Erasmus was once again without a home. He was no longer living like a poor church mouse; he now earned reasonably good money for his writing. In fact, the publication of *The Praise of Folly* three years earlier had won him undying fame in literary circles. He was not now about to return tamely to the monastery at Steyn. He wrote:

> I cannot see what I might do in Holland. I know that the climate and diet do not agree with me; and I should become the cynosure of all eyes, returning as a gray-haired old man, and in poor health too, to the place I left as a youth. I should be a target for the contempt of the lowest after being used to receiving honor from the very highest; I should exchange my studies for drinking parties.[44]

Erasmus could not resist boasting a little. Responding to Servatius's promise to find him a place of work that was suitable, Erasmus wrote, "I cannot guess what this could be, unless perhaps you are going to place me with some nuns, to be a servant to women, I who have never consented to be a servant, even to archbishops or kings!"[45]

Erasmus concluded, "Farewell, once my sweetest companion and now my reverend Father."[46] The last conciliatory words did not disguise the simple fact that Erasmus would never return to the monastery. He had become a man in the world, though perhaps not of it. He would continue to kiss the garments of the high and mighty while ridiculing their behavior in his witty letters and books.

## BASEL

In the spring of 1514, Erasmus set out on a leisurely journey down the Rhine River. He was headed for Basel, home of John Froben, his most recent printer and publisher. Along the way, Erasmus was feted by the townspeople of the German city of Strasbourg. He was astonished by the extent to which his fame had grown and by how well his works had been received.

In Strasbourg, Erasmus met and dined with Sebastian Brant, author of *The Ship of Fools*. The two men doubtless had much to say to one another, but no record exists of their conversation. Erasmus did, however, go further in his praise of Germany and the Germans than he had done in almost any other nation. He praised the people of Strasbourg and the city itself. This appeared to be a golden time, both for Erasmus and for his dearest hope, which was to bring a simple and serviceable piety to European life.

From there, it was on to Basel, where Erasmus worked closely with John Froben. Although Froben was not the man of letters and culture that Aldus Manutius had been, he was nonetheless an excellent publisher for Erasmus. Froben turned manuscript into printed material rapidly and in beautiful form. The two men's partnership would last for many years and would then be succeeded by Erasmus's relationship with John Froben the Younger.

Erasmus also made an enemy in Basel. He had worked for years on his translation of the Vulgate Bible, but he needed help in finishing his work. He had several assistants, one of whom was Johannes Oecolampadius. The two men were deeply attached to one another during the work, but they later had a falling out and became bitter enemies.

Froben printed Erasmus's *Novum Instrumentum*, the New Testament in Greek and Latin all in one elegant volume, in February 1516. Erasmus had taken some liberties with the text and had added many commentaries. There were critics, to be sure, but many people hailed the work as the greatest literary achievement of the past century.

Meanwhile, Thomas More was engaged in the greatest work of his lifetime. More labored away on his *Utopia*, while Erasmus polished and refined his translations of the Vulgate Bible. The

## UTOPIA

Thomas More's *Utopia* was published in 1516, the same year as Erasmus's New Testament. The two publications are often seen as the highpoint of the humanist movement in northern Europe.

In *Utopia*, which literally means "nowhere," More described an island called Utopia in the tropics. The island was about the same size as England, and the names and titles of the people seemed familiar, but it was there that the resemblance ended. In Utopia, the highest form of development was intellectual, rather than economic. People aspired to become more learned and more noble through the development of their minds. Utopia did not suffer from the social ills of England. More used Utopia as a way to describe the dislocations caused by land enclosure, sheep farming, and the growing separation between rich and poor in England. Perhaps he saved his most acute description for last when he described religion in Utopia. Utopus, the founder of the commonwealth,

> . . . Had heard that before his arrival the inhabitants had been continually quarreling among themselves. . . . From the very beginning, therefore, after he had gained the victory, he especially ordained that it should be lawful for every man to follow the religion of his choice, that each might strive to bring others over to his own, provided that he quietly and modestly supported his own by reasons.*

How much trouble might have been saved had England, France, Germany, and Spain done the same as Utopia in this regard!

* Kenneth J. Atchity, *The Renaissance Reader* (New York: HarperCollins, 1996), p. 113.

two great works both came out in 1516, a landmark year for literary studies in Western civilization.

*Novum Instrumentum* was published in February 1516, just a few months before Thomas More's *Utopia.* Erasmus's book, which was almost 600 pages long, carried a three-page dedication to Pope Leo X, who was apparently delighted. The text had Greek on the left side of the page and Latin on the right.[47]

The work was a massive accomplishment. Not only had Erasmus gone back to the original sources in Greek, but he had made adjustments between the Latin of Roman times and the Latin of his own day. Inevitably, though, there were questions and problems.

Erasmus rashly promised that if his critics could supply evidence to support their claims, he would amend the text. In his second and third editions, Erasmus corrected many mistakes, resulting in a final product that made him the first great biblical translator of his day.

# 7

# The Lutheran Challenge

"*Do not get angry. Do not hate anybody. Do not be excited over the noise which you have made. . . . Christ give you His spirit, for His own glory, and the world's good.*"

—Erasmus, in a letter to Martin Luther

E rasmus was at the top of his form in 1516 and 1517. He lived in Basel during these years, but he received frequent offers from kings, princes, and bishops to relocate. One of the most tempting came from a Sicilian bishop who offered an estate and money; a less enticing message came from the French King Francis I. To all these offers Erasmus responded in vague terms; sometimes he suggested that an author, like a Persian tapestry, is best appreciated from a distance. Eventually, he settled on the city of Louvain, located on the border between France and the Netherlands. Erasmus received honors and awards from the University of Louvain where he stayed from 1517 until 1521. Meanwhile, an enormous burden was finally and conclusively lifted from his shoulders.

Early in 1517, Erasmus received a dispensation from Pope Leo X. The pope absolved Erasmus of any penalties he might ever have incurred for deserting the monastic life and for failing to dress in a monk's clothing. Erasmus was now free to accept benefices (estates on a loan) from church leaders. For the first time in his life, Erasmus enjoyed a measure of financial security. With no serious rival, he was on top of the literary world.

There was also the opportunity to flatter and perhaps influence a new monarch. In 1516, Charles of Austria became King Charles I of Spain. To any perceptive observer, it was obvious that Charles would also succeed his grandfather Maximilian as Holy Roman emperor in the future (this happened in 1519). Erasmus received the honorary title of councilor to the 16-year-old Charles and was asked to write an essay in his honor. Erasmus took the opportunity to write *The Education of a Christian Prince*, which was published in 1516. Unlike Niccolò Machiavelli, who had published his *The Prince* in 1513, Erasmus tried to impress the need for modesty, good manners, and a yielding disposition for a true prince or king:

> You, too, must take up your cross, or else Christ will have none of you. "What," you ask, "is my cross?" I will tell you: Follow the right, do violence to no one, plunder no one, sell no public office, be corrupted by no bribes. To be sure, your treasury will

have far less in it than otherwise, but take no thought for that loss, if only you have acquired the interest from justice. While you are using every means and interest to benefit the state, your life is fraught with care; you rob your youth and genius of their pleasures; you wear yourself down with long hours of toil. Forget that and enjoy yourself in the consciousness of right.[48]

Erasmus meted out this sound advice in the year 1516, when he believed Europe was entering a new golden age. None of this peace and security was to last. Instead, he and others were to be disappointed by the bitter arguments over indulgences and the practices of the Catholic Church as a whole. It was Erasmus's fate to be an

## THE PRINCE

Niccolò Machiavelli published *The Prince* in 1513. It came out in a second edition in 1533 and has remained in print to the current day.

Readers generally are not comfortable with *The Prince*. They often disapprove of the theories Machiavelli proposed. The term "Machiavellian" has come to mean "cynical," "duplicitous," and "cunning." The great irony is that Machiavelli actually believed strongly in virtue. He thought that a prince (or king) needed to be strong and feared in order to coerce his subjects into being virtuous. The most oft-quoted section of the book comes in chapter 17:

All this gives rise to a question for debate: Is it better to be loved than to be feared, or the reverse? I answer that a prince should wish for both. But because it is difficult to reconcile them, I hold that it is more secure to be feared than to be loved, if one of them must be given up.*

Machiavelli has certainly been maligned as the "prince" of discord, when his actual purpose was to cultivate virtue in the Italian people so that they would resemble the Romans of old. Like Erasmus, Machiavelli wished his people to return to the standards of an earlier time.

* Allan H. Gilbert, trans., *The Prince and Other Works* (Putney, Vt.: Hendricks House, Inc., 1941), p. 145.

intellectual and a spiritual leader in a time of great change, and at least some of the demands for change would be directed at him.

## MARTIN LUTHER

Martin Luther, an Augustinian monk and priest, became increasingly disturbed by the presence of salesmen peddling indulgences. Upon investigation, Luther found that the indulgence salesmen were hard at work in Germany and elsewhere because Pope Leo X needed a great deal of money to finance the building of the new St. Peter's Basilica in Rome. Luther was not the only person upset by these events, but his voice was the loudest. When he shouted in 1517, all of Christendom heard his message.

On October 31, 1517, Luther pinned a series of statements on the church door in Wittenberg, Germany. Known as the Ninety-five Theses, the arguments were against indulgences and against the very concept behind them. How could the church, how could the pope, allow the common people to believe that salvation was for sale?[49]

At first, the church did not respond. Neither Pope Leo X nor his cardinals believed that this challenge from the German monk would come to very much. They were mistaken. The advent of the printing press meant that Luther's Theses were translated, printed, and distributed across Europe in a matter of months. Soon, Christians everywhere were discussing the matter of indulgences. Erasmus, too, would also be drawn into the discussion.

Erasmus had long condemned indulgences, but he had done so in parts and pieces of his books. He had never "taken on" the church establishment in the way Luther did. At first, Erasmus was content to remain on the sidelines and watch the process unfold. His sympathies may have been with Luther's cause, but the two men were so different in their approach and methods that it would be hard to see them coming together.

The crisis, however, continued to build. Luther became even stronger in his denunciations of the church, and the Catholic hierarchy responded with threats of its own. Jerome Aleander, who had been a roommate of Erasmus's at the home of Aldus

Manutius, was appointed the papal representative to deal with Luther and the spreading Lutheran heresy. Aleander and Erasmus had been good friends in those earlier times, but they now became bitter enemies.

Both sides—the Lutheran and the papal—pressed Erasmus to take a stand. He responded to both sides in the same way: He saw merit in some of what they said but not in all. Therefore, he could not choose sides.

## MEETING AT THE FIELD OF THE CLOTH OF GOLD

The early summer of 1520 witnessed an extraordinary combination of political meetings. Pope Leo X issued a papal bull, or decree, condemning Luther's beliefs and demanding that he recant within 60 days. At almost the same time, King Henry VIII of England and Francis I of France met in Belgium at a beautiful place near Calais. No French and English kings had met in such a peaceful fashion for 100 years, and the people of both nations were excited by the contrast between their handsome young monarchs. Henry VIII was just shy of 30. Six foot tall and broad-shouldered, he came to Calais intent on making an ally of King Francis I of France. If anything, Francis I was even more striking than Henry VIII. The French king was a tiny bit taller, and he wore enormous shoulder pads underneath his shirts, making him seem to be the largest man at his own court. Both Henry and Francis looked more like football players than kings.

The French arrived at the meeting place first and set up beautiful pavilions. The English came later and added flowers. The setting was so magnificent that people at once began to call it the Field of the Cloth of Gold.

In all the hurry and tumult of the event, it was easy to fail to notice Desiderius Erasmus. At age 54, he was about 20 years older than either of the two kings, and he had seen much more hardship in life than either of them. Erasmus had come on a special mission. He wanted to persuade King Henry to grant a hearing, and hopefully protection, to Martin Luther.

We know that Erasmus was brought to King Henry's pavilion and that the two men spoke with one another. We do not know what their conversation was like or anything about the arguments that Erasmus brought to bear. We are confident, however, that King Henry rejected Erasmus's request and refused to provide help for Martin Luther. Erasmus failed in his mission. Knowing as we do that Erasmus detested knights, cannons, and warfare, it is safe to surmise that he made his way from the encampment as soon as he could.

King Henry and King Francis entertained one another for the next week. There were numerous parties and exclamations of friendship. There was even a wrestling match between the two very physical monarchs: King Francis won. But neither king accomplished his aims. When they rode away after ten days of merriment, Francis had failed to bring Henry into an alliance with him against the king of Spain, and Henry had failed to persuade Francis to agree to cooperate with England. The Field of the Cloth of Gold had, for all its sumptuous magnificence, been an abject failure.

As Erasmus rode away, he may well have thought of some lines he had written seven years earlier. In his *The Praise of Folly*, he wrote of nationality and nationalism, which he considered one of the greatest follies of them all:

> Upon this account it is that the English challenge the prerogative of having the most handsome women, of being the most accomplished in the science of music, and of keeping the best tables. The Scotch brag of their gentility, and pretend the genius of their native soil inclines them to be good disputants. The French think themselves remarkable for complaisance and good breeding.[50]

Erasmus was correct in thinking that national pride was one of the downfalls of Christian consciousness. The question was whether he could awaken Europeans from their slumber before it was too late.

## RESPONSE TO MARTIN LUTHER

Just a few months earlier, Erasmus had met with George Spalatin and Frederick the Wise, Elector of Saxony (the seven electors chose the Holy Roman emperor). There was a long and passionate discussion, with Erasmus speaking in Latin, Frederick speaking in German, and Spalatin translating between the two. Erasmus defended Luther's right to speak his beliefs, however unpalatable they might be to the church. At the same time, Erasmus made it clear that he preferred harmony, especially in matters of religion.

Not long before, Erasmus had received his first letter from Martin Luther. The two men were destined never to meet, but they did exchange some correspondence between 1519 and 1522. Luther praised Erasmus as "our great hope" and asked him to declare for the Lutheran cause. Erasmus's answer was typically noncommittal:

> Had I not seen it with my own eyes, I could not have believed that the theologians would have gone so mad. It is like the plague. All Louvain is infected. I have told them that I do not know you personally; that I neither approve nor disapprove your writings, for I have not read them, but that they ought to read them before they spoke so loudly. . . . It was of no use. They are as mad as ever.[51]

Erasmus then tried to persuade Luther to be more moderate in his own words:

> Paul abolished the Jewish law by making it into an allegory; and it might be wiser of you to denounce those who misuse the Pope's authority than to censure the Pope himself. So also with kings and princes. Old institutions cannot be rooted up in an instant. Quiet arguments may do more than wholesale condemnation. Avoid all appearance of sedition. Keep cool. Do not get angry. Do not hate anybody. Do not be excited over the noise which you have made. . . . Christ give you His spirit, for His own glory and the world's good.[52]

Behind these gentle words was a consistent theme and message. Erasmus was his own man; he would not become Luther's tool or a mouthpiece for the pope or anyone else. Although many people of the time condemned Erasmus as a coward, he was far from it. True, he shrank from physical hardship and danger, but when it came to intellectual and spiritual matters, he stood his ground resolutely. He would not be forced into making a stand on the Lutheran issue.

Because of this resolute intellectual independence, Erasmus did not become a leader of the new Reformation movement. He remained on the sidelines. The world tends to remember Martin Luther much more than it does Erasmus because one year later, in the spring of 1521, Luther was called before the pope and the Holy Roman emperor and asked to recant his words. Luther refused, and in doing so became immortalized throughout history for his famous response "Here I stand; I can do no other." [53]

In the same year that Luther defied the powers of church and state, Erasmus fled from Louvain. He would not return to the Low Countries again.

# Ever the Wanderer

*"Now Basel farewell; no other city for many years has shown kindlier hospitality than you. I pray that hence forth everything will be happy for you, and that no less happy guest than Erasmus ever arrives!"*

—Erasmus, on his departure
from Basel, Switzerland

Erasmus had been uneasy at Louvain for some time. In August 1521, he wrote to a friend from Bruges:

> The Louvain friars will not be reconciled to me, and they catch at anything, true or false, to bring me into doom. True, my tongue runs away with me. I jest too much, and measure other men by myself. Why should an edition of the New Testament infuriate them so? I settled at Louvain, as you know, at the Emperor's order. We set up our college for the three languages [Greek, Latin, Hebrew]. . . . Then out came the Luther business. It grew hot. I was accused on one side from the pulpit of being in a conspiracy with Luther; on the other I was entreated to join him. I saw the peril of neutrality, but I cannot and will not be a rebel.[54]

Truly, Erasmus was never comfortable in one place for long. Although it is true that some of his colleagues at Louvain attacked him for what they believed were Lutheran sympathies, Erasmus also had good friends and colleagues on the faculty. Even so, he had made up his mind to leave Louvain and the Low Countries entirely. He headed to Basel in northern Switzerland, the home of his publisher, John Froben.

Erasmus took his leave most unexpectedly. He had to meet with his old friend and present foe, Jerome Aleander. The two met at the Inn of the Wild Man in Louvain and had a five-hour-long conversation. Knowing that he would soon be going away, Erasmus was much more daring than usual. He alternately taunted and played with Aleander. The latter was under strict instructions to be tactful with Erasmus, but he was so provoked that he once claimed the pope could do away with "one lousy writer" just as easily as with kings and queens. The very next day, Erasmus rode out of town on horseback. He and two servants kept riding until they reached the boundary of the Holy Roman Empire. Soon they turned south along the Rhine River, headed for Basel.

## LIFE AT BASEL

Erasmus had always experienced ill fortune in his choice of patrons. From the bishop of Cambrai in 1495 to the University at Louvain in 1521, he consistently found fault with his sponsors and they with him. Basel was an escape and more. The major attraction of the town was the presence of the printer and publisher, John Froben.

Froben had been expecting Erasmus for months. The publisher had even had a new open fireplace put in his home to welcome the famous author. Erasmus arrived after a journey of a week or so. He would remain in Basel for the next eight years, and it would become the closest thing he ever had to a permanent residence.

Even now there were dangers arising from the Lutheran controversy. Luther had given up on Erasmus, but some of Luther's followers persisted. They wanted to win Erasmus over to their cause, and they continued to make life difficult for him.

Erasmus settled into life at Basel. He was pleased with his new quarters, and might have been content had he not received a stream of visitors imploring him to take up with one side or the other in the Lutheran controversy. Erasmus was able to brush many of them off, but one special letter came from the new pope in Rome. Pope Leo X had died and was succeeded by Pope Adrian VI, a Netherlander whom Erasmus had known for many years; the two of them had been students together in Holland and had known each other as mature scholars at the University of Louvain. The new pope wrote in December 1522:

> It lies with you, God helping, to recover those who have been seduced by Luther from the right road, and to hold up those who still stand. Remember the words of St. James: "He that recalls a sinner from the error of his ways shall save him from death and cover the multitude of his sins." I need not tell you with what joy I shall receive back those heretics without need to smite them with the rod of the Imperial law. You know

how far are such rough methods from my own nature. I am still as you knew me when we were students together. Come to me in Rome. You will find here the books which you will need. You will have myself and other learned men to consult with, and if you will do what I ask you shall have no cause for regret.[55]

If ever there was an offer that Erasmus might accept, this was the one. He knew the pope and respected him both as a man and as a scholar. Erasmus also knew that Adrian was old and perhaps not well. What might happen if he went to Rome with papal protection only to find that Adrian had died and been replaced? Erasmus wrote back:

This is no ordinary storm. Earth and air are convulsed—arms, opinions, authorities, factions, hatreds, jarring one against the other. . . . [A]bove all, let no private animosities or private interests influence your judgment. We little dreamt when we jested together in our early years what times were coming. With the Faith itself in peril, we must beware of personal affections. I am sorry to be a prophet of evil, but I see worse perils approaching than I like to think of, or than anyone seems to look for.[56]

Erasmus would not go to Rome. Furthermore, Erasmus was correct in his fears. Pope Adrian VI died in 1523 and was succeeded by Pope Clement VII. Pope Clement was much less inclined to mercy than Pope Adrian had been, and relations between Catholics and Lutherans continued to deteriorate.

The worst was yet to come. In 1524, the great Peasants' Rebellion broke out in Germany. Thousands of peasants left their lands, burned their masters' houses, and set about to destroy whatever was in their path. The peasants believed that Martin Luther, who had had the courage to defy both the pope and the emperor, would be on their side. They were cruelly mistaken. Luther wrote essays to the German nobles, urging them to strike back at the rebellious peasants with all their might. The knights and princes did so, and Germany suffered a terrible bloodbath. As many as

100,000 people were killed (to learn more about this crisis, enter the keywords "peasants' revolt 1525" into any Internet search engine and browse the listed sites).

### ERASMUS TAKES A STAND

In 1524, at the urging of many of his friends, Erasmus finally took up his pen against Martin Luther. The issue he chose to dispute was the matter of the will. Luther had argued

## THE ITALIAN PAPACY

The Roman Catholic Church has had more than 300 popes in its long history. The vast majority of them have been native-born Italians.

Early in the history of the church, Italian churchmen were far more learned than their counterparts in other countries. Therefore, it made sense that Italians would generally take the throne of St. Peter and govern the church. As the centuries passed, and as Germany, France, England, and Spain came to have universities and learned men, they were not honored with having popes from their lands. Italians continued to dominate the College of Cardinals and to win the papal elections.

One of the brief interludes in Italian dominance came in 1521. Pope Leo X died and was succeeded by Adrian VI. A native of Holland and a fellow student of Erasmus from their childhood years, Pope Adrian appeared to be the best chance the Roman Catholic Church had for internal reform. Unfortunately, Adrian died in 1523 and was succeeded by Pope Clement VII, an Italian. From that day in 1523 until 1978, only Italians have held the office and throne of St. Peter.

In the autumn of 1978, a Polish cardinal was elected as Pope John Paul II. The new pope began a bold and forward policy of travel to different parts of the world. He became beloved by Catholic youth around the world and appeared to represent the best hope for expanding the church beyond its European base.

An assassination attempt on Pope John Paul in 1981 only served to make him more popular. He visited his would-be assassin in prison and converted him to the Catholic faith. Pope John Paul II, the first non-Italian pope for centuries, has been the most dynamic leader in the papacy for decades.

that people did not possess free will, that whatever they did proceeded from the way in which they had been made by God. Erasmus started from this point in his *On the Freedom of the Will*:

> Certainly I do not consider Luther himself would be indignant if anybody should find occasion to differ from him, since he permits himself to call in question the decrees, not only of all the doctors of Church, but of all the schools, councils, and popes; and since he acknowledges this plainly and openly, it ought not to be counted by his friends as cheating if I take a leaf out of his books. Furthermore, just in case anyone should mistake this for a regular gladiatorial combat, I shall confine my controversy strictly to this one doctrine, with no other object than to make the truth more plain by throwing together Scriptural texts and arguments.[57]

Erasmus, being a humanist, had a much more nuanced view of human will than did Martin Luther. Erasmus believed that people make the most of what tendencies they have, whether those tendencies are for good or evil. The main point is that no person, no matter how good or noble, actually wins God's grace. Instead, people, by doing the best they can, draw assistance from God and progress by grace to the next step. This very small addition of humans' voluntary work made Erasmus a believer in what we would today call "free will." Erasmus did his best not insist that his views should be held by all people, writing: "Truly—to conclude the argument—what such people choose to claim for themselves is their own affair. I claim for myself neither learning nor holiness, nor do I trust in my own spirit."[58]

This was the great difference between Erasmus and Luther. The latter believed and trusted in his own spirit. Erasmus, on the other hand, was willing to listen to opposing ideas as long as these were conveyed courteously:

I shall merely put forward with simple diligence those con-
siderations which move my mind. If anybody shall try to
teach me better, I will not knowingly withstand the truth. If
they prefer to rail at one who treats them with courtesy and
without invective, rather discoursing than disputing, who
will not find them lacking in that spirit of the gospel which
is always on their lips. . . . So that if they reply that Erasmus
is an old vessel, and is not capable of the new wine of the
Spirit which they offer to the world: if they really rate themselves so highly, let them at least treat us as Christ treated
Nicodemus and the apostle Gamaliel. Although Nicodemus
was ignorant, the Lord did not repulse him, because he
desired to learn.[59]

Luther took a year to respond to Erasmus, finally doing so in
his book *On the Bondage of the Will*. Luther's response, though
seemingly gentle, was actually quite cutting:

There are two reasons for this: first, your cleverness in
treating the subject with such remarkable and consistent
moderation as to make it impossible for me to be angry
with you; and secondly, the luck or chance or fate by which
you say nothing on this important subject that has not been
said before.[60]

This was damning Erasmus with faint praise! About 200 pages
later, Luther ended his argument by reiterating his belief that if
God is all-knowing, then nothing a man does happens without
God's consent, and therefore man does not possess free will:

I will here bring this little book to an end, though I am
prepared if need be to carry the debate further. However, I
think quite enough has been done here to satisfy the godly
and anyone who is willing to admit the truth without being
obstinate. For if we believe it to be true that God foreknows and
predestines all things, that he can neither be mistaken in his
foreknowledge nor hindered in his predestination, and that

nothing takes place but as he wills it (as reason itself is forced to admit), then on the testimony of reason itself there cannot be any free choice in man or angel or any creature.[61]

Here the matter rested. Neither Erasmus nor Luther was able to gain a victory in this battle of words. Thousands, indeed millions, of words have been written on the subject since.

## FAREWELL TO BASEL

As much trouble as he had with Luther, Erasmus found that he had another new foe in the religious arena. This was Ulrich Zwingli, the leader of a religious reform movement in Switzerland. Zwingli was, like Luther, against the pope and the Roman Catholic Church. Zwingli led the movement in Zurich that transformed the communion of the Roman Catholic Church into the Lord's Supper of the new Protestant faith. Like Luther, Zwingli believed in participation by lay congregation members in all aspects of church life. Unlike Luther, however, Zwingli had a great and lasting affection for Erasmus. For his entire adult life, Zwingli maintained that reading a particular section of one of Erasmus's books in 1516 had illuminated his belief in Christ's mercy.

Despite his admiration for Erasmus, Zwingli saw the great man of learning as a dangerous obstacle. Erasmus continued to counsel moderation, both in thought and in action, and leaders like Zwingli were infuriated by his refusal to take a stand. By 1529, Erasmus decided that Basel was too "hot" for him. He had a last meeting with another of his literary rivals, the compiler Oecolampadius, and then left the city, just as he had departed from Louvain after his meeting with Aleander. With him went his servant Margaret, who had been with him through thick and thin for many years. He often made fun of her manners behind her back, but claimed he would not replace her since he might end up with another servant who was even worse.

As Erasmus and Margaret took a boat up the Rhine River, the writer was applauded by the townspeople who had come to see him off. Their cheers melted his heart, and he composed a poem in their honor on the spot: "Now Basel farewell; no other city for many years has shown kindlier hospitality than you. I pray that henceforth everything will be happy for you, and that no less happy guest than Erasmus ever arrives!"[62] With these parting words, Erasmus headed north to Freiburg, Germany.

# 9

# Erasmus's Last Years

*You talk of the great name which I shall leave behind me,*
*and which posterity is never to let die. Very kind and*
*friendly on your part; but I care nothing for fame*
*and nothing for posterity. I desire only to go home*
*and to find favor with Christ.*

—Erasmus, in a letter
to Jacobus Latomus

rasmus arrived in Freiburg a day or so after his departure from Basel. A year later, he purchased a new house, the first he had ever owned in his life. He was as content materially as he had ever been.

Freiburg also afforded Erasmus protection. This was an imperial city, and no one could harm him without risking the wrath of Charles V, the Holy Roman emperor. As long as he stayed on the emperor's good side, Erasmus would be safe.

By now, about 1529, Erasmus had lost all hope of ever seeing European Christians united once more. In his lifetime, he had witnessed the corruption and laxity of the Universal (Catholic) Church, but he had never wished to see it fragment into separate Catholic and Lutheran groups.

Erasmus impressed the cause of peace on everyone he met. He had spent a life in the business of argument, disputation, and counterargument, but he called for a halt to all religious quarrels. Only when the different religious groups respected one another enough to allow for coexistence would peace be possible.

Yet even now, in the twilight of his years, Erasmus was not above a measure of revenge. When he learned that his two great foes in Basel—Zwingli and Oecolampadius—had both died, Erasmus wrote a letter that praised and applauded their demise. In a tone that was worthy of the worst that Martin Luther could summon, Erasmus thanked God for his mercy in allowing the two men to perish. Erasmus's words did much to keep the flame of religious hatred alive in Switzerland; they are justly viewed as one of his worst, or lowest, moments.

As always, there was more work to be done. Erasmus toiled at the new compilation of his *Colloquies* and continued to work on translations, but some of the heart had gone out of his work. It was no wonder. He had translated the New Testament from Greek into Latin with little real result in the behavior of the people. He had written *Conduct of a Christian Prince* but failed to influence European rulers. He had every right to be discouraged, both with his generation and himself.

## TROUBLE IN ENGLAND

Then came news from England. King Henry VIII wanted to cast off his wife, Catherine of Aragon, and wed one of her ladies-in-waiting, Anne Boleyn. Erasmus had long ago changed his mind about King Henry. The monarch by now was a far cry from the promising boy who had learned Latin so readily and shown such interest in the classics. As king, Henry had shown greater interest in war and conflict and tended toward becoming a tyrant. Erasmus was desperately afraid for his beloved friend Thomas More, who had agreed to serve as Lord Chancellor of England. Not that there had truly been any choice. One did not refuse such an honor, especially when it came from the hot-tempered King Henry VIII. So Thomas More, as Lord Chancellor, was now in the painful position of being asked to support King Henry's divorce.

Because Pope Clement VII had refused to grant a dispensation for a divorce, King Henry VIII had decided to take England out of the Roman Catholic Church and establish a new English Catholic Church, with himself at its head. As leader of the new church, he was able to get his divorce and soon married Anne Boleyn. King Henry was happy, the English people were not very upset, and only Queen Catherine had been dishonored. So why would Thomas More not simply allow this to occur?

More was younger than Erasmus, but the years since they had first met had made him more conservative. As he viewed the calamitous religious situation on the Continent, More was certain that he did not want to see the Roman Catholic Church fractured in England as well. He counseled Henry against the divorce and remarriage, and when his advice was scorned, More resigned as Lord Chancellor. He retired to his estate and spent time with his large family.

The years had wrought their changes on King Henry VIII as well. He had become more secretive, more malicious, and more vengeful. Rather than allow Thomas More to remain in peaceful seclusion, Henry insisted that the former Lord Chancellor swear to the Act of Supremacy, which formally established King Henry as the supreme lord of the new English Catholic Church. Thomas More did not openly defy the king, but he quietly refused to swear. As a result, he lost his head on the chopping block in July 1535.

Erasmus took the news of More's execution calmly, but this was the final straw that broke his heart. Of all the kings, princes, bishops, cardinals, popes, lawyers, nobles, and others he had known, he had loved only one person with all his heart: Thomas More. No one else had combined such gentleness of nature with such erudition and depth of mind. To see such a man beheaded because of a king's vengeance was just too much. Erasmus wrote to the bishop of Cracow, Poland:

> You will learn from a letter which I enclose the fate of Sir Thomas More and the Bishop of Rochester. They were the wisest and most saintly men that England had. In the death of More I feel as if I had died myself, but such are the tides of human things. We had but one soul between us.[63]

Little remained for Erasmus to do. He had spent his life in the cause of humanism, believing that the pursuit of *belles lettres* (good letters) would make a better world. Instead, he had seen the start of the Lutheran Reformation, a growing hatred between Catholics and Lutherans, and now the start of the English Reformation. One of his last letters was to Jacobus Latomus, written in August 1535:

> My life has been long if measured in years. Take from it the time lost in struggling against gout and stone, it has not been very much after all. You talk of the great name which I shall leave behind me, and which posterity is never to let die. Very kind and friendly on your part; but I care nothing for fame and nothing for posterity. I desire only to go home and to find favor with Christ.[64]

Things had changed dramatically. Many times in his life, Erasmus had longed for fame and attention. He had also seen how fragile these things are and how little they contributed to his overall level of happiness.

### "LORD SAVE ME, LORD LIBERATE ME!"

Erasmus was in great pain during the last two to three years of his life. He suffered, as he always had, from kidney stones, but he also had very bad arthritis. Weak as he was, he continued to stand at his lectern and write as much as he could. Still, the end was near.

It came in July 1536. One year after the execution of Thomas More, Erasmus uttered his last words: "Lord save me, Lord liberate me!"[65] The literary giant died in Basel.

In that same year and in that same town, a French lawyer brought out yet another of the "great books" of the Protestant

## ERASMUS'S HEALTH

He was, as they say, the creaking gate that lasts forever. Erasmus battled illness throughout his life and often felt he was about to succumb to his poor health.

One of his earliest battles came in his student days in Paris. He came down with a terrible fever and nearly died. For the rest of his life, he credited St. Genevieve, the patron saint of Paris, with his recovery.

At other times, Erasmus fled Paris for the Dutch countryside. He came close to death while he was in London, with the so-called "sweating sickness," and at least once in his life he probably contracted a low-level form of the bubonic plague.

The kidney stone was his greatest foe. He started to suffer from kidney stones in his thirties and the problem grew much worse as he aged. He suffered terribly from an attack while he was writing *The Praise of Folly*. At other times, his enemies complained that he must have had a stone when he wrote certain works, so severe were his words.

Erasmus survived. He bandaged his wounds, complained bitterly in letters to his friends, but soldiered on year after year. When he died in Basel in 1536, he had lived well into his late sixties, a very respectable age for the time and an excellent one for a person who had been weak and sickly throughout much of his life.

Reformation. John Calvin, who had left France for the relative safety of Switzerland, published his *Institutes of the Christian Religion.* The *Institutes* drew heavily on the writings of Martin Luther, but they went much further. Calvin asserted the doctrine of predestination, which means that God already knows, before a person has been born, whether his or her soul will eventually go to heaven or hell.

The theory or doctrine of predestination has been one of the most controversial aspects of Protestantism ever since. The followers of Martin Luther were known as Lutherans, and those who believed in Calvin's theory of predestination became Calvinists. It is fortunate for Erasmus that he died before having read the *Institutes* or becoming aware of how large a shadow they would cast over the entire Reformation.

At the time of Erasmus's death, the dream of a golden age for Christianity lay in tatters. Among them, Martin Luther, King Henry VIII, and John Calvin had created three new religious factions, which became known respectively as the Lutheran, Anglican, and Calvinist churches.

# 10

# The Individualist

*I cannot be other than what I am.*

—Erasmus

Erasmus's vision had floundered during a period of increasing suspicion and hatred. His ideal of a reformed Christianity had been wrecked by the controversies of Luther, Zwingli, Calvin, and others. Though Erasmus's hopes failed to come to pass, we must try to evaluate his life and career. How well did he do in the time allotted to him?

Erasmus grew up at a time and in a place where earlier virtues and wonders seemed to have disappeared. Erasmus spent much of his long life seeking out the Greek and Roman classics and looking for original editions of Plutarch, Livy, Jerome, and others. Erasmus saw the value of virtue and often urged younger men, in his letters, to cultivate it. Erasmus was most concerned with piety. This ideal was his touchstone.

Erasmus believed that the Catholic Church had strayed from its humble origins. In earlier times—say, the second and third centuries after Jesus—the Church had been small and based on local communities. There were no bishops or archbishops until about the third century after the death of Jesus.

Rightly or wrongly, Erasmus believed that this early time of the Christian Church had been a golden age and that he and his contemporaries could return to it through the practice of simple piety. This is why he never believed in indulgences. Even though he was never as harsh or aggressive as Martin Luther in attacking indulgences, Erasmus saw them as part of the rot that had accumulated on the Catholic Church over time. Erasmus wanted all Christians to practice simple piety as they had in the past.

Erasmus's relationship with Catholicism was complex. He had always loathed the strict practices of fasting, indulgences, and the like, but he believed there was much good in the Church that needed to be preserved. Therefore, when Martin Luther began to hammer at Pope Leo X and the hierarchy, Erasmus felt compelled to raise his voice in dissent.

The great similarity between Luther and Erasmus is that they were deeply pious men who were first and foremost individualists. Luther is famous for having said, "Here I stand; I can do no other." Erasmus often wrote, "I cannot be other than what I am."[66] As different as they appear, Luther and Erasmus shared this individualism in common.

Erasmus had the courage to write criticisms of the church long before Luther wrote his Ninety-Five Theses, but Erasmus was always conscious of his illegitimate birth and the fact that he had "escaped," as it were, from the Augustinian monastery.

Erasmus seldom achieved happiness, and when he did, it was almost always fleeting. He loved England in 1499, but left it for the Low Countries. He loved Venice, but exchanged it for Bologna. He lived in Louvain, but left it for Basel. There is a definite air of restless torment in his life. His literary works, in their great variety, reflect the wide breadth of his experiences and travels. From them, it is clear that he had many interests and a very capable intellect. He was a prolific writer, too, sometimes working as many as 14 hours per day.

Finally, Erasmus was always an individualist. Much as he yearned for the days of early piety and simplicity, he was actually too complex for such a world. He was, in truth, much closer to our modern world, with its complicated interconnections between politics, religion, and science, than he was to the days of the fathers of the Christian Church.

Erasmus was a man of many faces and a man of many words. Arguably, Erasmus was the greatest intellectual of the sixteenth century—and perhaps of any other.

# APPENDIX

### FROM *THE PRAISE OF FOLLY*: ON FRIENDSHIP

But perhaps there are some that neglect this way of pleasure and rest satisfied in the enjoyment of their friends, calling friendship the most desirable of all things, more necessary than either air, fire, or water; so delectable that he that shall take it out of the world had as good put out the sun; and, lastly, so commendable, if yet that make anything to the matter, that neither the philosophers themselves doubted to reckon it among their chiefest good. But what if I show you that I am both the beginning and end of this so great good also? Nor shall I go about to prove it by fallacies, sorites, dilemmas, or other the like subtleties of logicians, but after my blunt way point out the thing as clearly as it were with my finger.

And now tell me if to wink, slip over, be blind at, or deceived in the vices of our friends, nay, to admire and esteem them for virtues, be not at least the next degree to folly? What is it when one kisses his mistress' freckle neck, another the watt on her nose? When a father shall swear his squint-eyed child is more lovely than Venus? What is this, I say, but mere folly? And so, perhaps you'll cry it is; and yet 'tis this only that joins friends together and continues them so joined. I speak of ordinary men, of whom none are born without their imperfections, and happy is he that is pressed with the least: for among wise princes there is either no friendship at all, or if there be, 'tis unpleasant and reserved, and that too but among a very few 'twere a crime to say none. For that the greatest part of mankind are fools, nay there is not anyone that dotes not in many things; and friendship, you know, is seldom made but among equals. And yet if it should so happen that there were a mutual good will between them, it is in no wise firm nor very long lived; that is to say, among such as are morose and more circumspect than needs, as being eagle-sighted into his friends' faults, but so blear-eyed to their own that they take not the least notice of the wallet that hangs behind their own shoulders. Since then the nature of man is such that there is scarce anyone to be found that is not subject to many errors, add to this the great diversity of minds and studies, so many slips, oversights, and chances of human life, and how is it possible there should be any true friendship between those Argus, so much as one hour, were it not for that which the Greeks excellently call euetheian? And you may render by folly or good nature, choose you whether. But what? Is not the author and parent of all our love, Cupid, as blind as a beetle? And as with him all colors agree, so from him is it that everyone likes his own sweeterkin best, though never so ugly, and "that an old man dotes on his old wife, and a boy on his girl." These things are not only done everywhere but laughed at too; yet as ridiculous as they are, they make society pleasant, and, as it were, glue it together.

And what has been said of friendship may more reasonably be presumed of matrimony, which in truth is no other than an inseparable conjunction of life. Good God! What divorces, or what not worse than that, would daily happen were not the converse between a man and his wife supported and cherished by flattery, apishness, gentleness, ignorance, dissembling, certain retainers of mine also! Whoop holiday! how few marriages should we have, if the husband should but thoroughly examine how many tricks his pretty little mop of modesty has played before she was married! And how fewer of them would hold together, did not most of the wife's actions escape the husband's knowledge through his neglect or sottishness! And for this also you are beholden to me, by whose means it is that the husband is pleasant to his wife, the wife to her husband, and the house kept in quiet

A man is laughed at, when seeing his wife weeping he licks up her tears. But how much happier is it to be thus deceived than by being troubled with jealousy not only to torment himself but set all things in a hubbub! In fine, I am so necessary to the making of all society and manner of life both delightful and lasting, that neither would the people long endure their governors, nor the servant his master, nor the master his footman, nor the scholar his tutor, nor one friend another, nor the wife her husband, nor the usurer the borrower, nor a soldier his commander, nor one companion another, unless all of them had their interchangeable failings, one while flattering, other while prudently conniving, and generally sweetening one another with some small relish of folly.

# APPENDIX

**From *The Colloquies*: "Of Rash Vows"**

THE ARGUMENT. This Colloquy treats chiefly of three things.

1. Of the superstitious Pilgrimages of some Persons to Jerusalem, and other holy Places, under Pretence of Devotion.

2. That Vows are not to be made rashly over a Pot of Ale: but that Time, Expence and Pains ought to be employ'd otherwise, in such Matters as have a real Tendency to promote true Piety.

3. Of the Insignificancy and Absurdity of Popish Indulgencies.

ARNOLDUS, CORNELIUS

**Arnoldus.** O! Cornelius, well met heartily, you have heen lost this hundred Years.

**Cornelius.** What my old Companion Arnoldus, the Man I long'd to see most of any Man in the World! God save you.

**Arnoldus.** We all gave thee over for lost. But prithee where hast been rambling all this While?

**Cornelius.** In t'other World.

**Arnoldus.** Why truly a Body would think so by thy slovenly Dress, lean Carcase, and ghastly Phyz.

**Cornelius.** Well, but I am just come from Jerusalem, not from the Stygian Shades.

**Arnoldus.** What Wind blew thee thither?

**Cornelius.** What Wind blows a great many other Folks thither?

**Arnoldus.** Why Folly, or else I am mistaken.

**Cornelius.** However, I am not the only Fool in the World

**Arnoldus.** What did you hunt after there?

**Cornelius.** Why Misery.

**Arnoldus.** You might have found that nearer Home. Did you meet with any Thing worth seeing there?

**Cornelius.** Why truly, to speak ingenuously, little or nothing. They shew us some certain Monuments of Antiquity, which I look upon to be most of 'em Counterfeits, and meer Contrivances to bubble the Simple and Credulous. I don't think they know precisely the Place that Jerusalem anciently stood in.

**Arnoldus.** What did you see then?

**Cornelius.** A great deal of Barbarity every where.

**Arnoldus.** But I hope you are come back more holy than you went.

**Cornelius.** No indeed, rather ten Times worse.

**Arnoldus.** Well, but then you are richer?

**Cornelius.** Nay, rather poorer than Job.

**Arnoldus.** But don't you repent you have taken so long a Journey to so little Purpose?

**Cornelius.** No, nor I am not asham'd neither, I have so many Companions of my Folly to keep me in Countenance; and as for Repentance, it's too late now.

**Arnoldus.** What! do you get no Good then by so dangerous a Voyage?

**Cornelius.** Yes, a great Deal.

**Arnoldus.** What is it?

**Cornelius.** Why, I shall live more pleasantly for it for Time to come.

**Arnoldus.** What, because you 'll have the Pleasure of telling old Stories when the Danger is over?

**Cornelius.** That is something indeed, but that is not all.

**Arnoldus.** Is there any other Advantage in it besides that?

**Cornelius.** Yes, there is.

**Arnoldus.** What is it? Pray tell me.

**Cornelius.** Why, I can divert myself and Company, as oft as l have a Mind to it, in romancing upon my Adventures over a Pot of Ale, or a good Dinner.

**Arnoldus.** Why, truly that is something, as you say.

**Cornelius.** And besides, I shall take as much Pleasure imyself when I hear others romancing about Things they never heard nor saw; nay, and that they do with that Assurance, that when they are telling the most ridiculous and impossible Things in Nature, they persuade themselves they are speaking Truth all the While.

**Arnoldus.** This is a wonderful Pleasure. Well then, you have not lost all your Cost and Labour, as the saying is.

**Cornelius.** Nay, I think this is something better still than what they do, who, for the sake of little Advance-money, list themselves for Soldiers in the Army, which is the Nursery of all Impiety.

**Arnoldus.** But it is an ungentleman-like Thing to take Delight in telling Lies.

**Cornelius.** But it is a little more like a Gentleman than either to delight others, or be delighted in slandering other Persons, or lavishing away a Man's Time or Substance in Gaming.

**Arnoldus.** Indeed I must be of your mind in that.

**Cornelius.** But then there is another Advantage.

**Arnoldus.** What is that?

**Cornelius.** If there shall be any Friend that I love very well, who shall happen to be tainted with this Phrensy, I will advise him to stay at Home; as your Mariners that have been cast away' advise them that are going to Sea, to steer clear of the Place where they miscarried.

**Arnoldus.** I wish you had been my Moniter in Time.

**Cornelius.** What Man! Have you been infected with this Disease too?

**Arnoldus.** Yes, I have been at Rome and Compostella.

**Cornelius.** Good God! how I am pleas'd that you have been as great a Fool as I! What Pallas put that into your Head?

**Arnoldus.** No Pallas, but Moria rather, especially when I left at Home a handsome young Wife, several Children, and a Family, who had nothing in the World to depend upon for a Maintenance but my daily Labour.

**Cornelius.** Sure it must be some important Reason that drew you away from all these engaging Relations. Prithee tell me what it was.

**Arnoldus.** I am asham'd to tell it.

**Cornelius.** You need not be asham'd to tell me, who, you know, have been sick of the same Distemper.

**Arnoldus.** There was a Knot of Neighbours of us drinking together, and when the Wine began to work in our Noddles, one said he had a Mind to make a Visit to St. James, and another to St. Peter; presently there was one or two that promis'd to go with them, till at last it was concluded upon to go all together, and I, that I might not seem a disagreeable Companion, rather than break good Company, promised to go too. The next Question was, whether we should go to Rome or Compostella? Upon the Debate it was determin'd that we should all, God willing, set out the next Day for both Places.

**Cornelius.** A grave Decree, fitter to be writ in Wine than engrav'd in Brass.

**Arnoldus.** Presently a Bumper was put about to our good Journey, which when every Man had taken off in his Turn, the Vote passed into an Act, and became inviolable.

**Cornelius.** A new Religion! But did you all come safe back?

**Arnoldus.** All but three, one dy'd by the Way, and gave us in Charge to give his humble Service to Peter and James; another dy'd at Rome, who bade us remember him to his Wife and Children; and the third we left at Florence dangerously ill, and I believe he is in Heaven before now.

**Cornelius.** Was he so good a Man then?

**Arnoldus.** The veriest Droll in Nature.

**Cornelius.** Why do you think he is in Heaven then?

**Arnoldus.** Because he had a whole Satchel full of large Indulgencies.

**Cornelius.** I understand you, but it is a long Way to Heaven, and a very dangerous one too, as I am told, by reason of the little Thieves that infest the middle Region of the Air.

**Arnoldus.** That's true, but he was well fortify'd with Bulls.

**Cornelius.** What Language were they written in?

**Arnoldus.** In Latin.

**Cornelius.** And will they secure him?

**Arnoldus.** Yes, unless he should happen upon some Spirit that does not understand Latin, in that Case he must go back to Rome, and get a new Passport.

**Cornelius.** Do they sell Bulls there to dead Men too?

**Arnoldus.** Yes.

**Cornelius.** But by the Way, let me advise you to have a Care what you say, for now there are a great many Spies abroad.

**Arnoldus.** I don't speak slightingly of Indulgencies themselves, but I laugh at the Folly of my fuddling Companion, who tho' he was the greatest Trifler that ever was born, yet chose rather to venture the whole Stress of his Salvation upon a Skin of Parchment than upon the Amendment of his Life. But when shall we have that merry Bout you spoke of just now?

**Cornelius.** When Opportunity offers we'll set a Time for a small Collation, and invite some of our Comrades, there we will tell Lies, who can lye fastest, and divert one another with Lies till we have our Bellies full.

**Arnoldus.** Come on, a Match.

# CHRONOLOGY & TIMELINE

**1466**  Most historians consider this year as the probable date for birth of Erasmus.

**1469**  Some historians believe that Erasmus was born in this year.

**1483**  Thomas More is born.

**1487**  Erasmus takes monastic vows at Steyn.

**1491**  Henry Tudor, later King Henry VIII, is born.

**1492**  Erasmus is ordained a priest.

**1492**  Christopher Columbus arrives in the Bahamas.

**1493**  Erasmus enters the service of the bishop of Cambrai.

**1466**
Most historians consider this year as the probable date for birth of Erasmus.

**1500**
*Adages* is published.

**1487**
Erasmus takes vows as a monk.

**1460**          **1480**          **1500**

**1469**
Some historians believe that Erasmus was born in this year.

**1493**
Erasmus is hired as a secretary by the bishop of Cambrai.

**1494** Erasmus begins to study for his doctorate at the Sorbonne in Paris.

**1499** Erasmus goes to England with Lord Mountjoy.

**1499** Erasmus and Thomas More begin a lifelong friendship; Erasmus meets Prince Henry, later King Henry VIII.

**1500** Erasmus returns to Paris.

**1500** *Adages* is published for the first time.

**1503** *Handbook of the Militant Christian* is published in Paris.

**1506** Erasmus goes to Italy; receives doctorate at Turin.

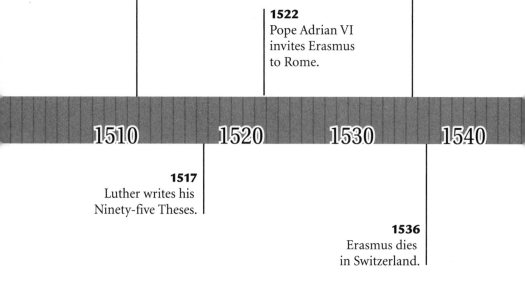

**1511**
*The Praise of Folly*
is published.

**1535**
Thomas More
is executed.

**1522**
Pope Adrian VI
invites Erasmus
to Rome.

**1510** **1520** **1530** **1540**

**1517**
Luther writes his
Ninety-five Theses.

**1536**
Erasmus dies
in Switzerland.

# CHRONOLOGY

**1507**  Erasmus visits Florence and Rome.

**1508**  Erasmus moves to Venice.

**1509**  Henry Tudor becomes King Henry VIII.

**1510**  Erasmus leaves Italy and returns to England.

**1511**  *The Praise of Folly* is published.

**1512**  *The Praise of Folly* is reprinted three times.

**1513**  Machiavelli's *The Prince* is published.

**1513**  Pope Julius II dies and is succeeded by Pope Leo X.

**1515**  Erasmus's *On the Education of a Christian Prince* is published.

**1516**  Erasmus's *New Testament* is published in Greek and Latin; Thomas More's *Utopia* is published.

**1517**  Erasmus settles at the University of Louvain; Martin Luther pens his Ninety-Five Theses.

**1518**  Erasmus's *Colloquies* is published for the first time.

**1520**  Erasmus meets Francis I and Henry VIII at the Field of the Cloth of Gold in Belgium.

**1521**  Martin Luther defies Emperor Charles V at Worms, Germany; Erasmus moves from Louvain to Basel, Switzerland.

**1522**  Pope Adrian VI invites Erasmus to Rome.

**1523**  Pope Adrian VI dies and is succeeded by Pope Clement VII.

**1524**  Erasmus's *Freedom of the Will* is published.

**1525**  Luther's *Bondage of the Will* is published.

**1529**  Erasmus leaves Basel for Freiburg.

**1530**  The Augsburg Confession results in an apparent truce between Lutherans and Catholics.

**1531**   Ulrich Zwingli dies.

**1533**   King Henry VIII marries Anne Boleyn.

**1534**   Pope Clement VII dies and is succeeded by Pope Paul III.

**1535**   Thomas More is executed by the order of King Henry VIII; Erasmus returns to Switzerland.

**1536**   Erasmus dies in Basel, Switzerland.

# GLOSSARY

**Adrian VI**—Roman Catholic pope from 1521 to 1523

**Aleander, Jerome**—Man of letters; papal diplomat against Lutheranism

**Basel**—A large town in Switzerland

**Bishop**—Person who governs a diocese of the Catholic Church

**Blount, William**—Lord Mountjoy; friend of Erasmus

**Bologna**—One of the Italian city-states

**Brabant**—Corresponded roughly to modern Belgium

**Cambridge**—One of the great English universities

**Canon**—Law of the Roman Catholic Church

**Cardinal**—One of the Catholic clergy officials responsible for electing the pope

**Catholic**—Literally means "universal;" until the Protestant Reformation, most Europeans belonged to the Catholic Church

**Charles V**—Holy Roman emperor and king of Spain, 1519–1556

**Church fathers**—Early Christians like Jerome, Origen, and Augustine

**Cleric**—Official of the Catholic Church, whether a priest or bishop

**Colet, John**—English humanist; dean of St. Paul's School in London

**Compostella**—Destination of one of the great pilgrimage trails

**Flanders**—A region in northern Europe; one-half lies in northern France; one-half lies in Belgium

**Florence**—One of the great Italian city-states

**Francis I**—King of France from 1515 to 1547

**Freiburg**—A city in southwestern Germany

**Froben, John**—Printer and publisher from Basel, Switzerland

**Gaugin, Robert**—French man of letters

**Henry VIII**—King of England who served 1509 to 1547

**Holland**—One of the Low Countries

**Holy Roman Empire**—Corresponded roughly to modern Germany

**Humanism**—The belief in the dignity and worthiness of man

**Italy**—There was no formalized Italian nation during Erasmus's life; the region consisted of the Papal States, Florence, Milan, Venice, and other independent city-states

**Julius II**—Roman Catholic pope; served 1503 to 1513

**Leo X**—Roman Catholic pope; served 1513 to 1521

**Louvain**—A Low Country university during Erasmus's time

**Low Countries**—The region of Europe now known as Holland, Belgium, and Luxembourg

**Luther, Martin**—German monk; leader of the Protestant Reformation

**Lutheran**—A follower of Martin Luther and his beliefs

**Machiavelli, Niccolò**—Italian man of letters; author of *The Prince*

**Manutius, Aldus**—Printer and publisher from Venice, Italy

**Milan**—One of the Italian city-states

**Monastic**—Referring to the monks and friars of the Catholic Church

**More, Thomas**—English humanist and statesman; beheaded in 1535

**Netherlands**—There was no organized nation of the "Netherlands" during Erasmus's time; the region was made up of the Low Countries, including Holland, Belgium, and Luxembourg

**Oecolampadius, Johannes**—Scholar who assisted Erasmus in translation of New Testament

**Oxford**—One of the great English universities

# GLOSSARY

**Papal States**—Middle parts of Italy; under control of the pope

**Reformation**—Literally, the process of reforming; usually applied to the Protestant Reformation, which began with Martin Luther in 1517

**Scholasticism**—Religious philosophy developed by St. Thomas Aquinas

**Scripture**—Literally "holy script;" usually applies to the Old and New Testaments and to some of the writings of the early church fathers

**Servatius**—Boyhood friend of Erasmus

**Sorbonne**—One of the great Parisian universities

**Strasbourg**—City on the Rhine; ownership disputed between Germany and France

**Switzerland**—Became independent around 1300; previously had been part of the Holy Roman Empire

**Venice**—One of the Italian city-states

**Vulgate**—The Bible, translated by Jerome; retranslated by Erasmus in 1516

**Winckel, Peter**—One of Erasmus's guardians

**Zwingli, Ulrich**—Leader of reform movement in Switzerland

# NOTES

## CHAPTER 1:
### Summons From England

1. R.A.B. Mynors and D.F.S. Thomson, *The Correspondence of Erasmus* (Toronto: University of Toronto Press, 1974), vol. 2, p. 147.

2. Ibid., pp. 147–148.

3. Ibid., p. 148.

4. Ibid., pp. 150–151.

5. Desiderius Erasmus, *The Praise of Folly* (New York: Dover Thrift Editions, 2003), p. 5.

## CHAPTER 2:
### Erasmus, His Brother, and the Brethren

6. R.A.B. Mynors and D.F.S. Thomson, *The Correspondence of Erasmus* (Toronto: University of Toronto Press, 1974), vol. 1, p. 5.

7. Ibid., p. 6.

8. Ibid., p. 2.

9. N. Bailey, trans., and Reverend E. Johnson, ed., *The Colloquies of Desiderius Erasmus Concerning Men Manners and Things* (London: Gibbings & Company, 1900), p. 56.

10. Ibid., p. 59.

11. Mynors and Thomson, vol. 1, p. 17.

12. Ibid.

13. Ibid.

14. Ibid., p. 41.

15. H. Bainton, *Erasmus of Christendom* (New York: Charles Scribner's Sons, 1969), p. 26.

## CHAPTER 3:
### Paris and London

16. Craig R. Thompson, trans., *The Colloquies of Erasmus* (Chicago: University of Chicago Press, 1965), p. 314.

17. R.A.B. Mynors and D.F.S. Thomson, *The Correspondence of Erasmus* (Toronto: University of Toronto Press, 1974), vol. 1, pp. 83–84.

18. Ibid., p. 193.

19. Ibid.

20. Ibid., pp. 235–236.

## CHAPTER 4:
### Venice and Rome

21. John P. Dolan, ed., *The Essential Erasmus* (New York: New American Library, 1964), pp. 28–29.

22. Ibid., p. 39.

23. Ibid., pp. 92–93.

24. Roland H. Bainton, *Erasmus of Christendom* (New York: Charles Scribner's Sons, 1969), p. 106.

## CHAPTER 5:
### The Praise of Folly

25. Desiderius Erasmus, *The Praise of Folly* (New York: Dover Thrift Editions, 2003), p. 5.

26. *Erasmus In Praise of Folly: With Portrait, Life or Erasmus, and His Epistle to Sir Thomas More* (New York: Peter Eckler, Publisher, 1910), p 25.

27. Ibid., p. 34.

28. Ibid., p. 55.

29. Ibid., p. 65.

30. Ibid., pp. 83–84.

31. Ibid., p. 98.

32. Ibid., p. 150.

33. Ibid., pp. 163–164.

34. Ibid., p. 197.

35. Ibid., pp. 197–198.

36. Ibid., p. 286.

37. Ibid., p. 292.

38. Ibid., p. 307.

## CHAPTER 6:
### The Wheel of Fortune

39. R.A.B. Mynors and D.F.S. Thomson, *The Correspondence of Erasmus* (Toronto: University of Toronto Press, 1974), vol. 2, p. 188.

# NOTES

40. H.C. Porter, ed., *Erasmus and Cambridge: The Cambridge Letters of Erasmus Translated by D.F.S. Thomson* (Toronto: University of Toronto Press, 1963), pp. 123–124.

41. Mynors and Thomson, vol. 2, p. 294.

42. Ibid., p. 295.

43. Ibid., p. 302.

44. Ibid.

45. Ibid.

46. Ibid., p. 303.

47. Desiderius Erasmus, *Novum Instrumentum* (Basel, Switzerland: John Froben, 1516).

## CHAPTER 7:
### The Lutheran Challenge

48. Lester K. Born, *The Education of a Christian Prince, by Desiderius Erasmus* (New York: Columbia University Press, 1936), p. 155.

49. Oskar Thulin, *A Life of Luther, Told in Pictures and Narrative by the Reformer and His Contemporaries* (Philadelphia: Fortress Press, 1966), pp. 30–33.

50. *Erasmus In Praise of Folly: With Portrait, Life or Erasmus, and His Epistle to Sir Thomas More* (New York: Peter Eckler, Publisher, 1910), pp. 163–164.

51. J.A. Froude, *Life and Letters of Erasmus: Lectures Delivered at Oxford, 1893–1894* (New York: Charles Scribner's Sons, 1894), p. 233.

52. Ibid., p. 234.

53. Thulin, pp. 30–33.

## CHAPTER 8:
### Ever the Wanderer

54. J.A. Froude, *Life and Letters of Erasmus: Lectures Delivered at Oxford, 1893–1894* (New York: Charles Scribner's Sons, 1894), p. 287.

55. Froude, pp. 308–309.

56. Ibid., p. 309.

57. E. Gordon Rupp, trans. and ed., *Luther and Erasmus: Free Will and Salvation* (London: SCM Press Ltd, 1969), p. 36.

58. Ibid., p. 46.

59. Ibid., p. 47.

60. Ibid., p. 102.

61. Ibid., p. 332.

62. Leon E. Halkin, *Erasmus: A Critical Biography*, trans. John Tonkin (Oxford, UK: Blackwell Publishers, 1993), p. 234.

## CHAPTER 9:
### Erasmus's Last Years

63. J.A. Froude, *Life and Letters of Erasmus: Lectures Delivered at Oxford, 1893–1894* (New York: Charles Scribner's Sons, 1894), p. 419.

64. Froude, p. 417.

65. Roland H. Bainton, *Erasmus of Christendom.* Charles Scribner's Sons, 1969, p. 272.

## CHAPTER 10:
### The Individualist

66. Roland H. Bainton, *Erasmus of Christendom* (New York: Charles Scribner's Sons, 1969), p. 283.

Ackroyd, Peter. *The Life of Thomas More.* New York: Doubleday, 1998.

Atchity, Kenneth J., ed. *The Renaissance Reader.* New York: Harper Collins, 1996.

Bailey, N., trans., and Reverend E. Johnson, ed. *The Colloquies of Desiderius Erasmus Concerning Men Manners and Things.* London: Gibbings & Company, 1900.

Bainton, Roland H. *Erasmus of Christendom.* New York: Charles Scribner's Sons, 1969.

Born, Lester K. *The Education of a Christian Prince by Desiderius Erasmus.* New York: Columbia University Press, 1936.

Dolan, John P., trans. *The Essential Erasmus.* New York: New American Library, 1964.

Faludy, George. *Erasmus.* New York: Stein and Day, 1970.

Froude, J.A. *Life and Letters of Erasmus: Lectures Delivered at Oxford, 1893–1894.* New York: Charles Scribner's Sons, 1894.

Halkin, Leon E. *Erasmus: A Critical Biography*, trans. John Tonkin. Oxford, U.K.: Blackwell Publishers, 1987.

Huizinga, Johan. *Erasmus and the Age of Reformation*, trans. F. Hopman. New York: Harper and Row, 1957.

Mynors, R.A.B., and D.F.S. Thomson, trans. *The Correspondence of Erasmus.* Toronto: University of Toronto Press, 1974.

Porter, H.C., ed. *Erasmus and Cambridge: The Cambridge Letters of Erasmus Translated by D.F.S. Thomson.* Toronto: University of Toronto Press, 1963.

Rilliet, Jean. *Zwingli: Third Man of the Reformation*, trans. Harold Knight. London: The Westminster Press, 1964.

Rupp, E. Gordon, and Philip S. Watson, eds. and trans. *Luther and Erasmus: Free Will and Salvation.* London: SCM Press, 1969.

# BIBLIOGRAPHY

Thompson, Craig R., trans. *The Colloquies of Erasmus.* Chicago: University of Chicago Press, 1965.

Zeydel, Edwin H. *The Ship of Fools by Sebastian Brant: Translated Into Rhyming Couplets With Introduction and Commentary.* New York: Dover Publications, 1944.

## PRIMARY SOURCES

Atchity, Kenneth J., ed. *The Renaissance Reader.* New York: Harper Collins, 1996.

Thompson, Craig R., trans. *The Colloquies of Erasmus.* Chicago: University of Chicago Press, 1965.

## SECONDARY SOURCES

Ackroyd, Peter. *The Life of Thomas More.* New York: Doubleday, 1998.

Bainton, Roland H. *Erasmus of Christendom.* New York: Charles Scribner's Sons, 1969.

Thulin, Oskar. *A Life of Luther, Told in Pictures and Narrative by the Reformerand His Contemporaries.* Philadelphia: Fortress Press, 1966.

## WEBSITES

The History Guide: Desiderius Erasmus
http://www.historyguide.com/intellect/erasmus.html

Desiderius Erasmus Resources at Questia
http://www.questia.com/popularSearches/desiderius_erasmus.jsp

MedievalChurch.org.uk: Desiderius Erasmus
http://www.medievalchurch.org.uk/p_erasmus.html

# INDEX

# INDEX

**SAMUEL WILLARD CROMPTON** lives in the Berkshire Hills of western Massachusetts. He was raised a Roman Catholic and is now a spiritual seeker. He has written a number of books on spiritual and religious topics; some of his biographical studies include *Martin Luther, Thomas Merton,* and *Emanuel Swedenborg.* Crompton teaches American history and Western civilization at Holyoke Community College. He is a major contributor to the *American National Biography,* published in 1999 by Oxford University Press.

**MARTIN E. MARTY** is an ordained minister in the Evangelical Lutheran Church and the Fairfax M. Cone Distinguished Service Professor Emeritus at the University of Chicago Divinity School, where he taught for thirty-five years. Marty has served as president of the American Academy of Religion, the American Society of Church History, and the American Catholic Historical Association, and was also a member of two U.S. presidential commissions. He is currently Senior Regent at St. Olaf College in Northfield, Minnesota. Marty has written more than fifty books, including the three-volume *Modern American Religion* (University of Chicago Press). His book *Righteous Empire* was a recipient of the National Book Award.